T0361115

ROUTLEDGE LIBRARY EDITIONS:
HISTORY OF MONEY, BANKING AND
FINANCE

Volume 5

AN EVALUATION OF FEDERAL RESERVE POLICY 1924–1930

AN EVALUATION OF FEDERAL RESERVE POLICY 1924–1930

CLAIRE HELENE YOUNG

Routledge
Taylor & Francis Group

LONDON AND NEW YORK

First published in 1992 by Garland Publishing, Inc.

This edition first published in 2018
by Routledge
2 Park Square, Milton Park, Abingdon, Oxon OX14 4RN

and by Routledge
711 Third Avenue, New York, NY 10017

Routledge is an imprint of the Taylor & Francis Group, an informa business

British Library Cataloguing in Publication Data
A catalogue record for this book is available from the British Library

ISBN: 978-1-138-70169-4 (Set)
ISBN: 978-1-315-10595-6 (Set) (ebk)
ISBN: 978-1-138-08982-2 (Volume 5) (hbk)
ISBN: 978-1-315-10896-4 (Volume 5) (ebk)

Publisher's Note
The publisher has gone to great lengths to ensure the quality of this reprint but
points out that some imperfections in the original copies may be apparent.

Disclaimer
The publisher has made every effort to trace copyright holders and would welcome
correspondence from those they have been unable to trace.

An Evaluation
of Federal Reserve Policy
1924 – 1930

CLAIRE HELENE YOUNG

GARLAND PUBLISHING, INC.
NEW YORK & LONDON
1992

Library of Congress Cataloging-in-Publication Data

Young, Claire Helene.
An evaluation of Federal Reserve policy 1924-1930 / Claire Helene
Young.
p.   cm. — (The Financial sector of the American economy)
Includes bibliographical references.
ISBN 0-8153-0960-0 (alk. paper)
1. Federal Reserve banks—History—20th century. 2. Banks and
banking—United States—History—20th century. 3. Monetary
policy—United States—History—20th century. I. Title. II. Series.
HG2563.Y85   1992
332.1'12'09730942—dc20   92-22999
                                                                CIP

Printed on acid-free, 250-year-life paper
Manufactured in the United States of America

CONTENTS

INTRODUCTION

Statement of Purpose

The purpose of this thesis is to explore the role of the Federal Reserve System in the Great Depression. Several theories of the causes of the Great Depression are commonly discussed. One, the Keynesian view, places deficient aggregate demand and a pessimistic attitude of business towards investment as causes and sustainers of the economic woes of the period from 1929 through 1945. Another view, that of monetarism, places monetary factors and the Federal Reserve System inadequacies as being largely responsible for causing and for aggravating the situation. This theory came into view in the 1960's after Milton Friedman had evaluated the monetary history of the United States. Other views of the depression combine the influences of both major theories.

What the Federal Reserve did, how they defended their actions, and how business writers, businessmen and economists viewed these actions are important. Analysis of those opinions should shed light on how aware of the appropriateness of Federal Reserve policy concerned participants of that time period were. Also, analysis of the opinions of business writers of the time regarding the general economic health of the country is an important foundation for understanding their evaluations. Accordingly, this thesis explores these areas in order that the thinking of the period may be better understood.

Organization

This thesis is divided into several chapters. The *Statement of Purpose* identifies the purpose of the work. CHAPTER I provides an historical background of the instabilities and strengths of the 1920's, an account of the stock market crash, Federal Reserve policy viewed retrospectively, and its impact upon banking and theories of the causes of the Great Depression. This section also provides background for understanding the consistencies and inconsistencies between what was believed to be correct policy then and (based upon the results of actual policy) what is believed now. CHAPTER II of this thesis is a year to year exploration of the writings of the day. Each year is analyzed in two sections. In each first section, titled "General Economic Conditions", a brief review of the events of the year is rendered. This is followed by an analysis of key writings from business magazines of that year which express opinions regarding the country's economic health. Each second section, entitled "Federal Reserve Policy", is also discussed in two stages. The first stage is an account of the Federal Reserve's policy and their justification for that policy. The second stage is comprised of the opinions of economists and businessman of Federal Reserve policy which were written either in that year or were written several years later about that year. The author notes connections between the perceptions of the day and actual results throughout the paper. The CONCLUSION analyzes on a year by year basis how well the opinions of the day conformed with reality. General conclusions about Federal Reserve policy and the astuteness of economists and business writers of the day are given.

AN EVALUATION
OF FEDERAL RESERVE POLICY
1924 – 1930

CHAPTER I

Historical Overview
The 1920's and the Great Depression

1. THE PROSPERITY OF THE 1920's

After the recessionary post World War I setback of 1920-1921, the twenties were characterized by rapid growth in productivity and overall income. The mood of the country was one of unbounded optimism and a feeling that prosperity was permanent. The depression that followed in 1929 shocked Americans and eroded faith in banking, the Federal Reserve System, and the future. So great was the shock that it took several years for the nation, businessmen, and economists to comprehend the gravity of the depression. It is important, therefore, to analyze the prosperity of the 1920's as well as the fundamental weaknesses in order to understand how disaster could strike such an unexpecting population.

During the 1920's a great investment was made in capital goods at the rate of about $17 billion per year. (1) Technological advances were rapid and productivity per worker underwent substantial increases. World War I had emphasized mass production and specialization benefits, and so post-war industrialists avidly studied the principles of scientific management as promoted by Frederick W. Taylor. Industries were also expanding rapidly (most notably durable consumer and investment goods, and, until 1926, construction). Residential construction increased so rapidly that by 1925, 937,000 units were started as compared to 405,000 units in 1919. However, this number would drop to 509,000 in 1929. (2) The building boom was due to population growth, rising incomes and building interruption during World War I. The automobile industry also grew very rapidly so that by 1929, twenty three million automobiles were registered compared to only eight million in 1920. A total of 4,795,000 automobiles were produced in 1929. (3) Prices for autos had dramatically dropped by 1926 from their 1903 level due to economies of large scale production. Other industries also prospered such as rayon, petroleum, radio, appliances, and chemicals, as well as manufacturing, retail distribution and food processing.

The rate of business consolidations from 1919 to 1929 was startling. In mining and manufacturing, there were 1268 consolidations. There were 270 consolidations in the iron and steel industries. (4) Over 1000 public utilities disappeared in 1926 alone as a result of consolidation. (5) By 1929, 49% of corporate wealth, 38% of business wealth and 22% of the nation's entire wealth was held by only 200 non-banking corporations. (6)

Furthermore, as a creditor nation after World War I who would not accept manufactured goods from foreign countries, the U. S. maintained a favorable balance of trade by making large foreign loans and investments abroad. From 1922 to 1929 an overflow from the U. S. of capital totalled $3.6 billion. (7) This trend continued until 1928 when American investors reduced their foreign loans, and exports of agricultural commodities and raw material substantially decreased. Therefore, until 1928 export trade contributed significantly to economic prosperity. (It was also, as we shall see later, a source contributing to the weakness of the economy.)

Another factor that contributed to the high level of prosperity of the times was the pro-business attitude of the government. (8) Because income taxes were reduced in 1924 and 1928, high income groups, business, and industry became the recipients of greater funds to invest. This stimulated rapid capital investment, but also, unfortunately, excessive stock market speculation. Herbert Hoover as Secretary of Commerce from 1921-1928, aided business as much as he could by promoting loans, exports, and protective tariffs. A laissez-faire attitude was taken towards government monitoring of business. In order to allow vast mergers, anti-trust laws were weakly enforced. Social welfare programs that would require higher business taxes or increase the prices of raw materials were vigorously opposed. Even federal public power projects were opposed until the 1930's.

The stock market was also undergoing acceleration as the 1920's were marked by mass speculation. Sensational schemes, narrow margins of 10%-20% (9) and other manipulations eventually drove prices of stocks up to unsustainable levels by late 1928. Yet, until that time, price increases were justified by increases in output in some industries.

During the 1921-1929 period, GNP increased 62% and $35 billion was invested in new plants and equipment for industry, agriculture, and commerce. Between 1920-1930, employment increased by 15% with one forth of this increase registered in non-farm sectors. (10)

In addition to this remarkable prosperity, the period from 1921-1929 is also notable for three other economic characteristics. (11) First, banks were undergoing important changes. Banks were engaging in side businesses such as distributing securities and fiduciary functions. Small town banks dwindled as agriculture became less important and as the automobile brought people to the cities. Second, when the gold standard was abandoned, the inexperienced Federal Reserve System had to develop monetary policy criteria. The result of this was that they attempted to draw upon their powers to promote economic stability. When economic conditions appeared to be favorable, they took credit for it. Third, towards the end of the 1920's a conflict over stock market speculation developed between the Federal Reserve Board and the Federal Reserve Bank of New York. This conflict indirectly contributed to the depressed economy of 1929-1932.

The change in banking and the development of Federal Reserve monetary policy were vital yet immeasurable factors in the boom of the 1920's. They were also integrally involved in the collapse of the system. This will be dealt with more in a later section devoted to the weaknesses of the 1920's.

2. PRICE STABILITY

Contrary to the usual expected inflation during a boom as demand accelerates, the prices of the 1920's were remarkably stable. Several explanations have been advanced for the stability. Wholesale

and consumer prices were less vulnerable from 1923 through 1929 than
in earlier periods.

Milton Friedman and Anna Schwartz in *A Monetary History of
the United States, 1867-1960* have proposed that the reason prices were
stable was that the quantity of money was kept more stable than it
otherwise would have been. They give the explanation that the
Federal Reserve would not allow gold flows to affect the quantity of
money. Therefore, prices were less variable because money was less
variable. According to Milton Friedman:

> "By 1923, wholesale prices had recovered only a sixth of their
> 1920-1921 decline. From then until 1929, they fell an average
> of 1% per year. The cyclical expansion from 1927 to 1929 is
> one of the very few in our record during which prices were a
> shade lower at the three months centered on the peak than at
> the three months centered on the initiation trough. The stock
> of money too failed to rise, even fell slightly during most of
> the expansion, a phenomenon not matched in any prior or
> subsequent cyclical expansion. Far from being an inflationary
> decade the 20's were the reverse. And the Reserve System far
> from being an engine of inflation, very likely kept the money
> stock from rising as much as it would have if gold movements
> had been allowed to exert their full influence." (12)

Price trends from 1920 through 1945 were extremely stable. (13)
Initially, after World War I prices declined and while stable from 1922
through 1929, there was slight price inflation in 1925 coincident with
the peak of the boom in construction.

Albert Niemi, in *U. S. Economic History* states that from 1815
on prices declined. He proposes this to be due to a decrease in the
velocity of circulation, the fact that money may have been held by
individuals who could not consume much of what they held, production
and technological increases, and some sort of international connection
as European price levels were similar. Dr. Niemi wrote, however, that
there was no absolute agreement on these factors or on the extent to
which they operated on price levels. Louis M. Hacker in *The Course of
American Growth and Development* also states that the stability in
wholesale prices, as well as a modest decline in consumer prices,
during this period was due to technological and productive advances.
(14)

It is reasonable to assume that as technological advances
increased production and further economies of scale were established,

prices would fall. Therefore, it seems logical to assume that with increased demand for products and increased supply at a lower cost, prices could be somewhat stable. Additionally, as shall be shown later, the 1920's were characterized by an unequal income distribution such that the most substantial income gains were in the domain of the top 1% of the population. Niemi's argument supports a view that these people had too much to consume with, thereby fueling securities investments instead of purchasing goods. Nevertheless, it must be mentioned that any increase in monetary income increased real wages (due to the stable prices) so that all classes benefitted somewhat from stable prices. This would create a downward pressure on prices as overall demand would be somewhat depressed. Furthermore, the argument of Friedman that the Federal Reserve restricted the variability of prices by restricting the variability of the money supply is important. Additionally, the low prices of farm products kept the cost of living to a manageable level for urban workers. (15) All of these factors, as well as the unexplained interconnection of European and American price levels, should account in some measure for the curious price stability of the period.

3. THE FUNDAMENTAL WEAKNESS OF THE 1920'S ECONOMY

The reason that the spirit of optimism in the 1920's would eventually be pierced by the Great Depression is that certain fundamental weaknesses existed in the economy of that time period.

John Galbraith in *The Great Crash 1929* cites five instabilities operating in the Twenties which will be listed and then discussed in length , in addition to several other weaknesses. (16) These are as follows:

(1)   Income was unevenly distributed so that the rich were very rich and so that the economy became dependent upon high levels of luxury consumer spending and/or high investment levels.

(2)   The corporate structure was weak having opened itself to frauds and swindlers, to holding companies which were over-leveraged, and to investment trusts. Businesses invested more in speculation than in production.

(3)   The bank structure was unstable as many loans were backed for collateral by goods whose prices subsequently would fall, and many of these loans were broker loans. Banks were weak due to the great number of independent banks, so that if one failed the result would be bank runs.

(4)   The foreign balance was in a poor state. Private loans were extended to debtor foreign nations by private American creditors. In the majority of cases, their terms were not worked out to protect the creditors. When tariffs prevented increasing exports, massive defaults occurred.

(5)   The economic intelligence was poor. (Later, a discussion of the weaknesses in Federal Reserve policy will demonstrate this.)

Additional sources of instability were the number of farm bankruptcies due to the weaknesses in the agriculture industry and hurting the holders of farm mortgages, stock market speculation, and the instabilities inherent in the construction industry. (17)

The following section is an analysis of these factors and how they worked to disrupt economic stability.

4. AGRICULTURE AND CONSTRUCTION INDUSTRY WEAKNESS

From 1897 until the end of World War II, agriculture boomed. When the war ended the demand for American products declined forcing prices down. Also, as immigration was slowed, consumption demand in the United States fell. Prohibition hurt the grain industry, and so did the fashionable dieting of women. (18) Therefore, even though production methods improved, demand slid. Furthermore, many marginal farmers could not afford the production capital. Gross farm income was reduced from $26.5 billion in 1920 to $10.5 billion in 1921. (19) Only modest gains were made from the latter year through 1929. Per capita farm income was $273 in 1929 compared to $750 as a national average. (20) The prices that farmers could receive for their products were substantially less than what they had to pay for the products they needed. Resultant farm bankrupcies and dissavings reduced the capital value of their property, and the share of agriculture in the national income declined.

The residential construction industry after 1925 was also weak. Real estate mortgage bonds furnished most of the money, and when the supply of housing filled post World War I needs (and as immigration fell), demand slackened. An industry that furnished 6% of employment during the boom and that was backed by speculation in bonds was in trouble. (21)

Beneath the boom, there were important industries with deep, troubled currents.

5. THE UNEVEN DISTRIBUTION OF INCOME

Even though the GNP grew at a rate of 6% between 1921 and 1929, gains in income were disproportionately allocated so that the very wealthy received most of the benefits. In point of fact, in 1920 the top 1% of the income bracket earned 13.64% of the total income, in 1925 they received 15.74%, and in 1929 they received 17.15%. In 1920 the top 5% of the income bracket earned 25.76% of the total income, in 1925 they received 30.24%, and in 1929 they received 31.88%. (22)

In addition to favorable tax laws, the top 1% of non-farm income households gained 97% in income. The lower 93% of the population gained only 6% during the period 1920-1929. Credit and installment buying by the lower strata overshadowed the imbalance in the 1920's. Furthermore, as mentioned earlier, with so much money in so few pockets, the demand for basic goods (less luxury items) would have to decline with income gains as one person can only consume so much bread. Much of the excess income of the wealthy naturally was fed back into investments. Therefore, a wealthy country was really a nation of a handful of very wealthy individuals. This weakness could cause important changes, so that healthy demand would decline causing a decline in capital investments and in supply.

This is summed up by Gilbert Fite and Jim Reese as follows: "From an economic standpoint, the distribution of income in the 1920's tended to increase the funds available for investment at the expense of funds available for consumer purchases." (23)

6. INVESTMENTS MADE BY BUSINESS

The beginning of the 1920's was characterized by large investments in capital goods. As mentioned earlier, tax laws were intentionally made favorable to encourage this. Yet toward the end of the 1920's, corporations provided more of the funds for speculation loans so that by 1929 they were the major source of such funds. They were engaging their funds in speculation, not production. Changes in demand structure due to the unequal income distribution caused surplus funds. The abnormally high profits to be made from loan interest caused business to invest these surplus funds in loans.

Thus, Fite and Reese stated:

"In retrospect, it now appears that more funds in the hands of consumers and less money in the hands of investors would have produced a more stable economy. While the stock market boomed, it was fed in part by bank credit. It was also a reflection of surplus investment funds which owners were not able to use profitably in the purchase of new equipment." (25)

7. STOCK MARKET SPECULATION AND FOREIGN INVESTMENTS

The spirit of optimism in the 1920's fed the stock market speculation. Over five years (1924-1929) The Dow Jones Industrial Average tripled and sales volume on the New York Exchange increased by 400%. (26) Brokers' loans supplied many of the funds and stocks were bought on margins as low as 10%. (27) The brokers' loans had collateral provided in the form of the stocks themselves and it was the banks (and towards the late Twenties the large corporations) who ultimately provided the funds. The increased income and tax savings of wealthy individuals and businesses fed the speculative fever. As mentioned earlier, until late 1928, price increases were indeed justified by increases in output. Broker loan interest was at 20% in May, 1929, as opposed to 12% in 1928. (28) By September, 1929, with common stock prices approximately 128% above price levels of 1926, an unsustainable plateau had been reached. (29)

As mentioned earlier, many large private loans were made to foreign nations which were not always protective of the creditor. From 1925-1929, $5 billion in foreign loans were raised in the United States for Europe and the rest of the world. (30) Many of these, particularly to Latin America and Germany, were unsound investments. The returns did not compensate for the very high risks associated with them. These loans were made because American investment houses and American investors who bought the bonds were inexperienced. Investments abroad skyrocketed from $3,514,000,000 in the year, 1914 to $ 17,009,000,000 in 1929. (31)

In addition to these factors, stock market speculation was aided by the flood of new securities created by the merger wave of the 1920's. In an ill-fated attempt to diversify risk, investment trusts became popular wherein managers bought securities of existing companies from money put in by investors. Real estate bonds for a construction industry that would sag in 1926 were also popular.

All of this created a very weak foundation for investments with values, that in the emotional heat of the rush towards wealth, blew up so rapidly that they bore no reasonable relationship to their real worth.

8. THE INSTABILITY OF BANKING (1920-1929)

As mentioned earlier, the constitution of loans and the great number of independent banks caused structural weakness in the banking industry.

The period from 1920 through 1929 was one of change in banking. Both the number and the size of banks as well as the nature of credit operations changed dramatically. Security loans increased from 33% to 38% and real estate loans increased from 14% to 17%. By 1929 commercial loans had fallen to 45%. (In 1914, commercial loans were 53%.) While in 1914, bank investments were at 32%, they swelled to 40% from 1922-1929. (29) This was due to a large number of consumer loans, buying of government securities, and direct security purchases. Bank organized "affiliates" enabled banks to both wholesale and retail stocks and bonds. First these "affiliates" issued the bonds, preferred stock, and common stock. Then they bought some of it for a speculative increase. Fiduciary functions (as the

Federal Reserve relaxed trust function limitations) increased.   (33)
Also, foreign securities were publicly floated in mass.   All of this
depicted a change from bank loans to stocks and bonds in order to
raise funds, and a qualitative erosion of credit outstanding.   In the late
1920's loans had a higher default rate than the loans of earlier days as
undue optimism for repayment allowed bankers to ignore credit
quality.   High risks were not adequately compensated for by high
returns.   These factors created disturbances in the banking system.
Where from 1914-1921 the number of banks increased from 27,000 to
30,000, they had declined to 25,000 by 1929. (34)

The first banking failures were linked in an earlier discussion
to weaknesses in the agricultural sector.   The failure rates of
commercial banks in many instances was among bank towns with
populations of 2500 or less and capital of less than $25,000. (35) The
failures first came in seven agricultural states. The absence of deposit
insurance would lead to panic and subsequent runs on other banks
(which will be discussed later) as depositors' fears of loss became self
fulfilling prophesies.

According to Milton Friedman, the banks made a reasonable
wager and the 1929-1933 collapse was neither foreseeable nor
inevitable. Just as the Federal Reserve was inexperienced in matters
of speculation, so was the banking system. Real gains in productivity
must have enticed them into making the loans and purchases that they
did. As will be shown later, Federal Reserve policy was instrumental
in translating the initial havoc of the banking problems into disaster.
The banks may appropriately be labeled inexperienced bettors in
speculative matters in the first instance, and victims in the disastrous
chain of events which occurred from 1929 through the trough of the
depression, March, 1933. Yet it is difficult not to point to some of
their activities in the later 1920's and regard them as careless, as they
did abandon caution and become involved in low quality, high risk
consumer and broker loans. By engaging in more security and
consumer loans as well as stock and bond transactions and fewer
commercial loans, they, with the businesses themselves, turned
dangerously from production to speculation.

9. THE COURSE OF FEDERAL RESERVE POLICY IN THE 1920's

From 1920-1921 the gold reserve position controlled monetary policy. Yet as the "Tenth Annual Report" of 1923 stressed, new criteria were needed to replace the gold reserve ratio. (36) Open market operations were recommended as the credit policy tool, and in 1922 the Open Market Commission was formed. How to use the tool was a matter left unanswered with only the suggestion to encourage productivity instead of speculative uses. Since the depression of 1920-1921 had roots of disturbances in speculation in commodities, the inexperienced Federal Reserve Board only understood dangerous speculation to mean commodity speculation. The open market operation and discount rate tools were not understood by the Board. Without real knowledge, the Federal Reserve Board pursued the onerous burden of promoting economic stability in the 1920's. In order to understand the effect of their actions, it is necessary to trace them in relation to Friedman's three factors that account for changes in the money stock. These factors are high-powered money, the deposit-reserve ratio, and the deposit-currency ratio. (37) High-powered money equals publicly held currency plus deposit liabilities to banks by the Federal Reserve System plus vault cash. The deposit-reserve ratio equals the ratio of commercial bank deposits to bank reserves. The deposit-currency ratio equals the ratio of commercial bank deposits to publicly held currency.

Except for the 1923-1924 and the 1926-1927 recessions, deposit-ratios and high-powered money rose in the 1920's. From 1921 through 1929, the money stock rose 45% total and was the cumulative result of a 54% increase in the deposit-currency ratio, a 15% rise in the deposit-reserve ratio, and a 27% increase in high-powered money. The growth of high powered money slowed between 1925 and 1927 as did the money stock. The deposit-reserve ratio rose mainly as "reserves held fell relative to the reserves required". (38) The rise in the deposit-currency ratio is attributed to the rise in real income per capita. The increased deposit-reserve ratio permitted banks to make deposit holding more attractive than currency.

After 1923, there was an inverse relationship between high-powered money and gold. The Federal Reserve System did this purposely, stating that with the gold standard temporarily gone, gold could not be used as an equilibrium force. Yet when the period after 1925 brought reinstitution of the gold standard, the Board continued the practice of "sterilizing" gold flows. (39) (Eventually, the gold standard was again dropped as countries overvalued their money resulting in depressed conditions.) Had gold flows been allowed to effect the quantity of money, there would have been greater variability in high-powered money, real income, and prices. Economists today believe that this "sterilization" process contributed to the major movement of gold out of this country in 1931. While "sterilization" may have contributed to stability in the 1920's, by the end of that decade it caused instability. This is because after the 1925 return to the gold standard, had gold been allowed to effect the quantity of money, stabilizing forces would have started that eventually would have ended the cycle. (40)

In order to understand what the Federal Reserve did with its non-gold monetary policy, an analysis of high-powered money is in order. Three distinct movements of money are important. First, in 1923-1924 the growth of high-powered money fell. This was because the discount rate had been raised and government securities were being sold as price inflation in 1922 began to cause concern. Federal Reserve credit fell, offsetting a sizeable gold inflow from 1923-1924, and causing a decline in high-powered money. This mild recession then led to a reversed policy (lowering the discount rate and raising government security holdings) so that high-powered money rose. The Federal Reserve credit decline followed by a rise "offset gold flows so that the net effect on high-powered money was slight". (41) As deposits to currency rose in 1927, the money stock changed more than high-powered money causing a retardation in 1926 and a rise in 1927. In part this was due to the Federal Reserve obliging requests for easy money by France, England, and Germany. Benjamin Strong, Governor of the New York Federal Reserve Bank, and a man supposedly vehemently opposed to inflation, aided it by actively endorsing these requests. In 1928 the Board tried to restrict the stock market boom by raising the discount rate to 5% and by selling government securities. (42) (Yet later they opposed raising it to 6% at the insistence of the Federal Reserve Bank of New York.) Discount rates fell relative to rapidly rising market rates so that banks now had a stronger incentive to borrow from the Federal Reserve System. The stock market boom therefore was blamed on the policy of easy money in 1927. The easy money was simply used to buy common stocks thereby fueling further speculation. It is believed today that the bull market could have been broken earlier if restrictive measures had been taken in 1927. The restrictive measures of 1928-1929 (including raising the discount rate to 6% in August, 1929) caused wholesale prices to decline, but not the stock boom. The end result was that the policy was not strong enough to hurt business. Milton Friedman stated:

"The bull market brought the objective of promoting business activity into conflict with the desire to restrain stock market speculation. The conflict was resolved in 1928-1929 by adoption of a monetary policy not restrictive enough to halt the bull market yet too restrictive to foster vigorous business expansion." (43)

Kenneth Galbraith, in *The Great Crash 1929* also commented on the Federal Reserve Board's actions:

"Such is the mystique of central banking. Such was the awe-inspiring role in 1929 of the Federal Reserve Board in Washington, the policy-making body which guided and directed the twelve Federal Reserve Banks. However, there was a jarring difficulty. The Federal Reserve Board those times was a body of startling incompetence." (44)

The tragedy is not without a human element. One reason the Board would not take restrictive measures earlier was that the new Federal Reserve Bank had requested them not to do so. Locked in an embittered feud over raising the discount rate to 6%, the Board refused to budge until it was too late. Later, as we shall see, as the battle accelerated, the Board would refuse to commence open market operations during the depression because the New York Federal Reserve Bank had requested it. Important men such as Charles Mitchell, a Director of the New York Federal Reserve Bank and President of the National City Bank, saw it in their own interest to perpetuate the boom which is precisely what they did.

According to Milton Friedman:

"After a break in stock prices on March 25, 1929, Charles E. Mitchell ...announced that his bank was ready to lend $25 million on the call market "whatever might be the attitude of the Federal Reserve Board"...to avert a sharper price decline." (45)

Therefore, the struggle to prove oneself right greatly intensified the problems. Finally, it is important to point out with respect to Federal Reserve policy an important view held by Galbraith in *The Great Crash 1929*. According to Galbraith, even if the Federal Reserve had decided to pursue open market operations, they had only $228 million of government securities in 1928 to sell. (46) This would have had only a slight restraining effect on the acceleration. Not only did they not conduct such operations, but by buying acceptances they gave commercial banks, now relieved of the burden, more with which to speculate.

In conclusion, the Federal Reserve Board was an important factor in turning what could have been a recession into a major depression. By trying to develop their skills in controlling our economy, they moved in opposite directions from where they should have been. Once gold flows had been sterilized, they did not have an adequate monetary policy to follow. Not only was the sterilization process harmful in and of itself, but their easy money policies and delayed reactions were very damaging. They failed to curtail speculation in 1928 once they knew that security speculation was indeed dangerous. The Federal Reserve Board only curtailed productive investments, the very type of investment they believed necessary. The Board's bickering with the New York Federal Reserve Bank prolonged the bull market, turning a problem into a nightmare. Later, as we shall see, they would prolong the depression and crush the banking system with further inaction.

10. SUMMARY

To summarize, the prosperity of the 1920's was being slowly undermined by fundamental weaknesses in the economy. These weaknesses included problems in certain key industrial sectors such as agriculture and construction, as well as poor corporate structure, income inequality, poor quality of foreign loans, excessive speculation in the stock market, and a low level of economic intelligence. The banking industry and the Federal Reserve System underwent fundamental changes in the 1920's which reinforced both the hopes of the times as well as the impending disaster. In short, the foundation of prosperity was weak, and long before the stock market crash of 1929 forces were gathering to injure the economy.

11. THE GREAT DEPRESSION

In early 1929 the United States had most of the world's real income and wealth, and the view of the future was bright. Yet from October, 1929, until 1933, the United States suffered the greatest economic contraction of modern days. Furthermore, the contraction became international in scope. During this period, net national product (in current prices) fell more than 50%. Net national product in constant prices fell more than 33%, implicit prices plunged more than 25%, and monthly wholesale prices fell by more than 33%. (47) Consumer prices fell 20.6%. (48) Gross National Product in constant dollars slipped more than 30%. (49) One third of commercial banks disappeared due to liquidations, consolidations, and mergers. The former confidence in the Federal Reserve System's omnipotent powers vanished. The rapid decline in prices created a decline in income of 36% over the four year period. The employment picture was devastating with one out of four persons unemployed. During the worst years, 1932-1933, unemployment averaged 24%. (50) Non-whites and those in capital goods producing industries were hit the hardest. Overall, there was a decline of 39% in employee compensation. Velocity of circulation fell by 33%, which was less than expected. The smaller than expected decline was because the bank failures so characteristic of the depression made it unattractive to deposit money, and therefore, less was saved in the form of deposits than would ordinarily have been. The money stock fell by 35% as a result of the interactions among the declines in the deposit-currency and deposit-reserve ratios (37% and 20%, respectively), and the 17.5% rise in high-powered money. (51)

Some types of output fell more than others. Gross private domestic investment for capital goods fell 89%. There was an 82% decline in residential construction, 75% in other construction, 67% in producers' durable equipment, 50% in consumer durable goods sales, and 15% in non-durable consumer goods sales. National income was down 54% during these four years. Hardest hit were manufacturing, which fell in net income by 65%, farm proprietorships which fell by 68%, mining which fell by 89%, and contract construction which fell by 83%. (52) Farm prices fell to 44 from an index of 100 with a low parity of 58. (53) Farm mortgage foreclosures doubled during this period.

With output severely down and gross national income and employment compensation also down, 50% of rental income was gone and there was a 62% decline in the income of proprietors of unincorporated businesses. (54) Business failures increased by 50%. Due to the large pre-depression investments, great amounts of outstanding debt totalling $190.9 billion had accumulated by 1929. As prices and income fell, the debt burden was magnified and wide sweeping defaults occurred.

Decline in a few businesses would trigger a chain reaction of declines starting with depressed demand for productive equipment and new construction. Excess capacity was thereby created, lowering new capital investment profitability. This deflation of prices and incomes reduced savings which hurt banks, thereby reducing their liquidity and solvency and causing them to restrict loans. Business recovery would be extremely difficult due to excess capacity, large unsatisfied amounts of debt, and loss of credit worthiness.

By the mid 1930's, the depression was of a worldwide scope. The Soviet Union was the only major country to escape economic depression due to its policies of economic independence, "autarky". Prices fell as well as employment, and one unfortunate consequence was the rise to power of the Nazis out of Germany's desire to unite and rise up out of the trough. International trade fell, severing those trading mechanisms which linked countries. The volume of international lending declined for the same reasons it slowed in the United States. The gold exchange standard was abandoned by one European country after another from 1930-1933. However, monetary trade mechanisms were not established. This was because countries tried to become economically isolated thereby restricting trade via such measures as import tariffs. This severely hampered international tade.

12. THE STOCK MARKET CRASH

Earlier, we identified not only the sources of prosperity but the weaknesses which caused the catastrophe described above. It is now necessary to identify the line of demarcation from riches to rags: the stock market crash of 1929.

While the weaknesses in the economy were worsening before the great crash, the stock market crash was the beginning of the long downward trend. The crash was as emotionally charged and dramatic as it was damaging. On October 10, 1929, a decline in prices on the New York Stock Exchange began, causing a general panic by October 24, 1929, which was reflected in an avalanche of trading. This avalanche amounted to the trading of 13 million shares. Behind this crash were the extremely high stock prices (128% above the 1926 price levels) which meant low yields. When combined with decreased economic activity and a rise in the interest rate to 20% for broker and dealer loans, the bullish market turned bearish. October 23-24, 1929, were the days when the stock market completely crashed. (55) Production, wholesale prices, and personal income began to fall, and so the stock market crash was both a symptom of the economic problems and a force that would deepen it. After the stock market crash, consumers and businesses were unwilling to spend, thus pushing income down. As a result, greater quantities of money were held. Business appeared to be unprofitable to the public and the already harmful contraction of business loans for productive uses was magnified.

After the crash, New York banks took over the loans of brokers and dealers (approximately $1 billion) and other loans as well (approximately $300 million). (56) Those parties accepted deposits in the New York banks as repayment. The New York banks did not pressure borrowers for repayment immediately, and this is why demand deposits increased greatly shortly after the crash. This forced the deposit-reserve ratio down for the United States overall, and the New York banks had to acquire additional reserves by borrowing from the Federal Reserve Bank of New York. These actions were prudent and timely in that they prevented an erosion of confidence in the banks and increased money market rates. Yet in the month after the crash, the deposit-currency ratio and high-powered money fell, depressing the stock of money. From August, 1929, through October, 1930, the deposit-currency ratio rose 7% leaving the system vulnerable to the bank runs which followed. While the discount rate fell, discounts declined because money interest rates were falling even faster. Discounting became unattractive. (57)

13. BANK FAILURES AND
THE FEDERAL RESERVE ATTITUDE

Contrary to the feeling of the Federal Reserve that small non-member banks were not a part of the system and could not hurt it, the bank failures of November, 1930, led to panic elsewhere. These failures, caused by the terribly bleak agricultural picture, now led to the failures of 352 banks by December, 1930. (58) When the Bank of the United States failed, the panic worsened because even though this was a private bank it was considered by the public to be "official" by virtue of its name.

The public began to hold more currency and banks paid out their reserves. This depletion of reserves would set off other failures, and the Federal Reserve took a passive stance. By January 31, 1931, deposits again rose and the first crisis was ended. (59)

One source of great trouble was that with the crisis, government bonds became more desirable as banks sought liquidity and dumped their lower grade corporate bonds. This caused government bond yields to fall, corporate bond prices to fall, and yields to rise leading to a reduction in the bond portfolio value of banks. This would contribute later to bank failures.

During the first crisis, the deposit-currency and deposit-reserve ratios fell as did the money stock. (High-powered money did rise, however, due to an increase in Federal Reserve credit outstanding, and this weakened some of the effects of the crisis.) At the end of the first crisis, the money stock rose a bit causing increased confidence in the banks and a rise in the ratios. However, after December 30, 1930, the Federal Reserve System again "sterilized" gold flows and exerted a contractionary influence.

With limited Federal Reserve credit outstanding and a money stock of only 1% higher in March than in January, 1931, a second banking crisis developed. (60) Furthermore, the economic decline that the United States touched off in Europe caused reverberations back in the United States. Corporate bond prices continued to fall and the Federal Reserve credit outstanding did not change so that the second banking crisis was worse than the first. The problem climaxed on September 21, 1931, when Great Britain abandoned the gold standard and many foreign countries exported their gold in the United States back home. (61) At the same time depositors withdrew currency from banks, and a series of additional bank failures followed. From August, 1931, through January, 1932, 1860 banks suspended operations. The deposit decline caused the money stock to fall by 31% during this time frame. The gold drain and the rise in discount rates intensified the difficulties dramatically. Had the gold export been accompanied by open market purchases, the gold drain could have been offset. However, the Federal Reserve did nothing. Banks then borrowed from the Reserve System and sold their assets on the market to meet currency demands and to make up for gold exports. From August, 1931, to January, 1932, high-powered money rose by $330 million, but publicly held currency rose by $720 million. ($390 million of this was from bank reserves.) Unwilling to draw down reserves in order to free this $390 million, the banks had to apply a multiple of 14 so that deposits fell by $14 for each $1 withdrawn by the public. This was a multiple contraction of deposits. (62) This multiple contraction of deposits led to disastrous results which could have been avoided if banks had been provided with more high-powered money.

Eventually, bank failures tapered off, reserves were bolstered, and the money stock fell at a slower rate. This action was the result of the Federal Reserve finally purchasing government securities, and through these open market operations infusing the tired economy with funds. These purchases were stopped, however, in January, 1933. A third banking panic followed not to be remedied until after a series of banking "holidays" wherein bank obligations did not have to be met. In this third crisis, the Federal Reserve System raised the discount rate but did not accompany it by open market operations. This left banks again with the one option of liquidating their securities, further devaluing their portfolios.

President Roosevelt created banking holidays from March 6-15, 1933, and suspended gold shipments abroad and gold redemptions at home. All told, 5000 bank failures occurred. From January to March, 1933, the money stock fell 12%. The deposit multiplier rose from 14 to 29 so that for every $1 made available to the public, deposits had to contract by $29 in order to keep the same reserve ratio. (63) The enormity of the second and third collapses is thought to be the result of banks with weakened capital positions unable to withstand even minor drains. Another part of the picture was the fact that the Reconstruction Finance Corporation (RFC) made public the names of banks borrowing from it, causing runs on those banks. With the new Roosevelt administration, a fearful public, not knowing what monetary policies the administration would follow, was ready at the smallest reverberation to convert deposits into currency. For the first time, the third run was characterize by demand for gold coin and certificates reinforcing the external gold drain.

The lack of deposit insurance was another major cause for these runs. Deposit insurance was one of the major reforms to come out of the depression.

The usual four sources of funds which banks have in order to meet claims have been identified by Chandler in *America's Greatest Depression 1929-1941*:

"(1) inflows of savings, (2) receipts of interest and promised payments of principal on its investments, (3) sale of assets from its portfolio, and (4) borrowing from others." (64)

As income and prices fell during the depression, savings and repayments also fell so that these two normally sufficient sources were unavailable. Sale of assets was a poor option as the flood of assets onto the market depressed their prices. Borrowing from the Federal Reserve was out of the question for non-member banks, and those who could borrow found that the credit available was sorely inadequate.

Two aspects of the bank failures are very important. First, the loss of capital to owners and depositor was an obvious difficulty. Second, the Reserve System policy allowed the failures to cause a vast decline in the money stock. The failures themselves had a cost of $2.5 billion which was a small fraction of the $85 billion worth of stock values on the New York Stock Exchange at that time. (65) However, deposits fell $18 billion which, as the deposit-currency ratio fell, caused the money supply to fall. The Federal Reserve, by not infusing more high-powered money into the banks so that a multiple contraction of deposits would not occur, gave the decline in the money stock the greatest momentum.

The attitude of the Federal Reserve was that the bank failures were due to problems in bank management and not to their own actions. They failed to draw the "connection between bank failures, runs on banks, contraction of deposits, and weaknesses of bond markets". (66) The Federal Reserve System had no feelings of responsibility to non-member banks. They did not care when the first banks failed because they were "rural" and consequently of little interest to the urban pinnacle of the system. Because of the infighting between the Federal Reserve Board and the New York Federal

Reserve Bank, when the bank asked the board to conduct the needed open market operations, the board refused. The conflicts between these two entities became an economically deleterious force. Continuing the pre-depression tradition, the Federal Reserve System by its actions both deepened and prolonged the depression.

14. THEORIES OF THE GREAT DEPRESSION

We carefully have reviewed the events that occurred before and during the depression. There is no clear agreement whether demand or the Federal Reserve failed first.

According to the Monetarists, the depression was caused first by sterilizing gold flows and contracting loanable funds when they should have been expanded. Rural bank runs from poor agricultural crops then began the bank runs which were, as we saw, worsened by the unhelpful Federal Reserve. Open market operations were helpful, but were abandoned too quickly, and the depression continued to its trough in 1933.

According to the "Spending Hypothesis" of Peter Temin and the Keynesians, the depression was the result of changes in aggregate demand. This caused employment, output, and money stock to fall.

Depressions are always characterized by a fall in income, consumption, and investment. Certain factors made the 1930 depression more severe and of greater duration than those in 1921 and 1938. Not only did investment fall in the 1930 depression, but so did consumption which rose in 1921 and then fell sharply in 1938. Exports also fell dramatically, where they had not before. Investment composition differed in 1930 from other periods as construction was much lower and inventory much higher. Construction fell largely due to a fall in income in the 1930's and this seriously affected the economy's health. The construction lag from 1926-1929 was due to depressed demand as immigration had been cut back and World War I demand had been satisfied. The construction decline triggered investment declines. The fall in consumption was due, in part, to the stock market crash in that the crash caused a decrease in personal wealth and changed expectations. Of the two explanations, Temin feels that changed expectations about future prosperity were the more likely vehicle of a decrease in consumption. At what point in time the change in attitude from optimism to pessimism occurred is at issue, but a commonly held notion is that the dividing line was the stock market crash. Public declarations continued to be positive. As late as November, 1929, Business Week called the depression a business recession. By December, reports were similarly optimistic stating that the worst would be over within six weeks. Other articles presented either pessimistic or optimistic forecasts of the future. It was not until the last quarter of 1930 that opinion changed. It took approximately one year after the crash for business opinion to change. The fact that "a smaller proportion of bonds were downgraded in 1930 than in either 1921 or 1937 demonstrates beyond a shadow of a doubt that the bond rating agencies did not expect a major depression in 1930". (67) It appears that bond rating agencies, while aware of the fact that business was not good, expected it to recover as quickly as it had in 1921. Overall, the fall in consumption remains unexplained. In discussing this, Peter Temin in *Did Monetary Forces Cause the Great Depression* said:

"It is somewhat unsatisfactory to say that the Depression was started by an unexplained event, but this alternative is preferable to statements that are inconsistent with the data. The spending hypothesis is consistent with the data if we accept the autonomous nature of a large part of the fall in consumption in 1930. It is not, however, a complete story." (68)

15. CONCLUSION

Both factors in these theories seem to have played an important role in the onset of the Great Depression. It seems logical that both the inaction and the misguided action of the Federal Reserve System did allow the bank runs. It is also logical to assume that the inaction of the System was largely responsible for the stock market acceleration and crash, as the System refused to break the bull market when it was manageable. Fundamental demand problems also hurt the economy. These fundamental problems may be traced to income inequalities which fed speculation but not consumption of sufficient consumer goods. These factors are also traceable to the post crash desires to withdraw money and save it in a mattress rather than to spend it or to deposit it. Naturally, once the ball was rolling, lack of income and employment would seriously hamper demand. Therefore, the depression may have been the result of soft-line or nonmonetarism theories. According to Gordon and Wilcox:

> "Soft-line monetarism: monetary and/or nonmonetary forces could have initiated the downturn; however, once started, the decline in the money supply and associated bank failures converted a serious recession into a major depression... Soft-line nonmonetarism or Keynesianism: according to this view, nonmonetary forces played the primary role in the downturn and contraction; however, monetary forces clearly aggravated the situation and deepened the depression. This view recognizes the failure of the Federal Reserve to function as lender of last resort." (69)

As Dr. Cargill states in "The Great Depression and the Keynesian-Monetarist Debate", the hard line nonmonetarist view that nonmonetary sources were responsible for the Great Depression is unfounded. (70) The Federal Reserve did fail as a lender of last resort. However, which soft-line view is correct is still a matter of debate.

A most interesting aspect of this is why it took so long for the experts and the public to recognize the problem. Not only were the fundamental weaknesses of the 1920's passed over, but even when the depression became an active economic condition public denial was rampant. Undoubtedly, some of this was due intentionally to try to break the panic. Nevertheless, lack of recognition of these problems is an interesting phenomenon which merits more attention. Accordingly, this thesis will next explore both widely published business articles and professional journal articles of the economists from 1924-1930. Emphasis will be given to writings dealing with the most complex policy controlled aspect of the Great Depression: Federal Reserve Credit Policy.

CHAPTER II

Opinion of the Period
Economic Conditions & Federal Reserve Policy

1. GENERAL ECONOMIC CONDITIONS (1924)

The period from 1923-1924 was characterized by a recession and wholesale prices that declined slightly. While industry was somewhat slack overall, residential construction gained 22,000 units (to 893,000) and automobile registration increased by approximately 2.2 million (to 15,436,102). (71) Of particular interest is the fact that 1924 was the last year of the great 1920-1924 gold flows. It is important to analyze what was written at that time regarding economic conditions and the policy of the Federal Reserve System.

On February 22, 1924, B. C. Forbes presented an optimistic view of the future. (72) It was Mr. Forbes' opinion that business should improve as he felt that money rates were cheap and would increase business investments. He pointed out that, due to the gold inflows, the Federal Reserve was not being called upon for loans and that their earning assets had declined from over $3 billion to under $1 billion. The gold inflows were creating this effect as well as weakening interest rates in many of the major cities.

Also, Forbes cited the fact that capital expenditures for roads, construction, railroads, and public improvements were very high. He felt that the lowering of income taxes would stimulate new business. If Coolidge was elected, he asserted that new business strength would be found. Considerable buying in the securities market showed economic strength, and improvements in the steel, oil, and agricultural industries were just around the corner. For business overall, Forbes said: "As I see it the probabilities are strongly for improvement." (73)

Mr. Forbes optimistic outlook continued and on December 15, 1924, he published an article in which he discussed his findings. (74) Without passing judgment, Forbes alluded to the unusually large purchases of securities on the stock market. He also discussed the very high level of business activity in basic industries such as iron, steel, and automobiles, concluding that the expected improvement in business had indeed materialized. While cautioning that inflation or labor difficulties could set the nation back, Forbes concluded:

"Without question, there is room for business to increase a good deal more without raising apprehensions or justifying the applying of any breaks by the Federal Reserve Banks." (75)

As far as speculation was concerned, John Moody informed his readers in Forbes Magazine of dramatic trends. (76) He asserted that the nation had become a nation of investors with literally thousands supplying capital for large productive investment. The investor class had grown greatly in size and it was no longer confined to the very rich. Moody warned, however, that speculative disasters characterize corporate development. He believed that the nation's growth had brought with it speculative movements of riotous proportions. Mr. Moody concluded that speculation in worthless securities had reached alarming totals and that the American investor was too confident. A line of demarcation between speculation and investment was his final recommendation.

As was discussed in CHAPTER I, a fundamental weakness of the 1920's was the high rate of rural bank failures which would, in the late 1920's, begin a series of banking panics. Popular opinion on the subject, though rather sparse, is an important variable to examine particularly as to whether or not the Federal Reserve System should have saved these banks. As will be shown later, the Federal Reserve did not see any need to assist these banks with their difficulties, and neither did Forbes Magazine. In an article entitled "Truth About Bank Failures in the Northwest", March 1, 1924, (77) Mr. Oakwood chastised those who blamed these failures on the inadequacies of the Federal Reserve System. Proof of this blame was evidenced on notices posted on banks with statements such as:

"This bank is forced to close because of inadequate temporary aid from the Federal Reserve Bank in order to meet the constant temporary withdrawals of deposits occasioned by fright on account of the widespread bank failures in the State." (78)

Mr. Oakwood argued that the Federal Reserve should not serve as a catch all for bad loans. He felt that the agricultural conditions were too poor to sustain the tremendous credit outflow to farmers made necessary by such conditions. In North Dakota, South Dakota, Minnesota, and Montana credit peaked at $1.3 billion on June 30, 1921, from $544 million in 1913. Each of the four states had more banks than were needed or sustainable, and the rural loans could not be met. According to Mr. Oakwood, bad bank management allowed these poor loans and this should be the problem of the banks and not the Federal Reserve. President Coolidge agreed in his statements that government agencies should not be responsible for loans by banks with unsecured collateral. Mr. Oakwood stated:

"It is possible to indulge the hope that out of this experience there may come an improvement in the management and policies of the financial institutions which serve the agricultural interests." (79)

Therefore, business readers of the day were told to expect healthy business conditions which by the end of the year did indeed materialize. Caution regarding inflation, labor, and over-speculation was evident, and the Federal Reserve System was staunchly defended in its lack of support for rural banks.

2. FEDERAL RESERVE POLICY (1924)

Federal Reserve credit reserve policy in 1924 was partly a function of sterilizing large European gold flows. In the Federal Reserve Bulletin of 1924, the Federal Reserve Board discussed the gold inflow situation. (80) According to the Federal Reserve, gold imports were commonly deposited by the member banks so that they could be counted as part of their legally required reserves, reduce discounting, or increase reserves and hence lending power. The influx of gold from the middle of 1922 came after a period of business expansion when loan credit demand was high. Accordingly, the member banks used the gold to expand credit with rediscounting, so that they became more independent of the Federal Reserve Banks. This caused concern within the Federal Reserve, as they were the organization charged with maintaining a good credit situation and ensuring that this country would not be harmed when and if gold poured out as Europe returned to the gold standard. Gold inflows were expected to slow. By July, 1924, they had.

The resulting impact of this logic was a rise in the discount rate and a decrease in high-powered money in order to neutralize or "sterilize" gold flows. However, the 1923-1924 recession caused a reversal in policy later in the year. By September, 1924, money rates had declined to 3 1/4% from the 5 1/2% of a year earlier. (81) This slackening of money rates was the result both of the gold inflows and the reduction of the discount rate from 4 1/2% to as low as 3%. (82) Also contributing were the open market operations of 1924 in the form of the purchase of government securities which were intentionally executed in order to permit member banks to repay indebtedness to the reserve banks. The Federal Reserve defined these operations:

"At the time when the open market purchases were made there was a recession in industrial activity, the attitude of the business community was hesitant, and there was no evidence of the growth of speculation." (83)

The policy was followed in the spirit of complying with the "Annual Report of 1923" which held as a goal the accommodation of business and commerce.

According to the Federal Reserve, one apparent result of this was that, due to the lack of demand to finance current business:

"Surplus funds accumulating at the banks have been transferred in part to the financial centers, where they have sought employment in loans on collateral and in the purchase of securities." (84)

Member credit was high as banks invested the easy money in loans on securities as well as their own investments. Gold imports were also used as the basis to lend money for stocks and bonds and to purchase investment securities. The 1923-1924 recession appeared to begin speculative activity, with surplus easy money funds not in demand for business being channeled rapidly into the securities market. From May through August, 1924, member bank stock and bond loans increased by $400 million and security investments by $375 million.

In conclusion, the Federal Reserve had kept discount rates high during the first part of 1924 in the interests of sterilizing gold inflows, which effectively were promoting member bank independence of the system. In compliance with their own "Annual Report of 1923" in which credit policy tools were first adopted, easing measures were taken when recessionary conditions became evident. By their own admission, the Federal Reserve recognized that the easy money which they had created was being funnelled into security speculation as business was still unwilling to borrow most of it for direct capital expenditures. Unfortunately, when speculative activity was even greater, they would not remember this lesson.

The public reaction to this was a chiding by businessmen when discount rates were relatively high, and a divided opinion among bankers. (85) Again, when credit was eased, opinion was divided. In general, bankers and industrialists feared that inflation could be the end result. Easy wealth was feared by bankers as they viewed the common man of insufficient means ill equipped to speculate successfully. As the earlier cited articles show, the overall tenor was a positive regard for the future with some fear of inflation. A somewhat skeptical group of critics seemed pleased on the whole with the movements of the Federal Reserve System.

Another problem which plagued the Federal Reserve was that of politics. The infighting between the Federal Reserve Board and the Federal Reserve Bank of New York led to a refusal on the part of the Board to restrain credit in the late 1920's. Apparently, politics in general dominated the Board, prompting grave concern by a former member of the Board, Mr. Paul Warburg. As early as 1923, Warburg warned that the political pressures placed on the Reserve Board were "threatening in the future the gravest consequences to the business stability and safety of the nation." (86) With all of the demands of politicians, he asserted, competent men refused to sit on the Board. Warburg further contended that valuable members of the Board were dispossessed of their posts when they had displeased Senators. In his opinion, no expert bankers sat on the Board.

According to the opinion of this insider, the net result was that the policies promoted so gingerly by the Federal Reserve System were being executed by political appointees operating in an environment of political control. The predispositions of such a group must have influenced the policy of easy money which began in 1924.

3. GENERAL ECONOMIC CONDITIONS (1925)

A brief review of the economic conditions of 1925 reveals that prosperity was in full swing. Residential construction had peaked at 937,000 units (a gain of 44,000 units) and automobile registrations had increased by approximately 2 million (to 17,439,701). (87) The year was also characterized by a slight inflation in wholesale prices, an end to the vast gold importation of 1920-1924, and easy money policies with discount rates between 3 1/2% and 4%. However, speculation and foreign loans were accelerating rapidly. Also, the agriculture industry was still in poor condition and the upper income brackets were receiving an increasingly disproportionate percent of the gains made in national income.

Opinion regarding economic conditions as expressed by business writers changed over the course of the year.

By early 1925 the attitude was that the sustained advance in security values was justified and would be followed by sound advances in business. (88) (As mentioned in CHAPTER I, many of the increases may indeed have been justified by output.) As small lots of stocks were being purchased by a great many individuals, it was also believed that there was nothing to fear from pools of speculators.

By the fall of 1925 the speculative fever was fully recognized. B. C. Forbes informed his readers in Forbes Magazine that the speculation was the result of unlimited credit. (89) Forbes already expressed the fear that with stocks at such an unprecedented height, a small calling of loans would initiate rapid selling. He felt that business was in better condition than the stock market. Forbes also proposed the idea that with the current bullish attitude and rapid advances in business, the speculative pace would become more rapid as caution had been abandoned.

In a later article on October 1, 1925, "Business and Stock Market Very Happy - Will It Last?", Forbes summarized the healthy business conditions. Housing, automobiles, oil, and other industries were doing well, and while not expected to last, even agriculture showed a slight improvement. Underwriters had so many clients buying securities that they could not find enough offerings to satisfy them. Yet, under the glorious surface, Forbes was still suspicious and he concluded the article with words of doubt:

"Yet, notwithstanding all this the writer has an uneasy feeling that the more speculative divisions of the stock market have become more vulnerable and that it would be unsafe to count too confidently upon nothing but bullish happenings in the business world. Is there not danger that people are indulging in too rosy expectations? If prudence be exercised all round this country should enjoy active, healthy, and rationally profitable business. But if a boom be fostered, then watch out." (91)

Another writer felt that the prosperity was here to stay. In November, 1925, Mr. John Oakwood, also writing in Forbes Magazine, addressed the issues of speculation, easy money, and economic conditions in "Are the Days of High Money Rates Gone Forever?" (92) Eight factors were held accountable for the current conditions. First, by enlarging and pooling money more efficiently the Federal Reserve assured an ample supply of money for business demands. Second, through the discount market, bank funds were increased as commerce received additional funds. Third, more gold than needed was in the credit structure. Fourth, business had surplus funds of their own which could be used internally either to finance operations or for speculation. Fifth, low money rates were also due to the federal debt reduction of $4 billion over the last five years. Sixth, rapid inventory turnover created strong cash positions for firms, who then needed to borrow very little. Seventh, with bank deposits up, banks could invest these surplus funds in the purchase of securities. Eighth, the cautious, price sensitive consumers, while buying quite a bit were also saving, causing business to react with similarly cautious buying. Oakwood's opinion of his analysis was that low money rates were here to stay and that "in the long view it means continued prosperity and greater aggregate benefits." (93)

However, while Oakwood was satisfied with his view of a prosperous future, Forbes continued to warn readers of a more gloomy horizon. In December, 1925, Forbes stated:

"The writer cannot but feel that multiplication has been carried so far that the stock market position has become a source of danger. Never before were such gigantic amounts of stock bandied about by speculators of unlimited daring and having access, apparently, to unlimited credit. Turnover has exceeded all former records... The time is coming when something will hit the market a blow from which it will not so readily recover." (94)

4. FEDERAL RESERVE POLICY (1925)

According to the Federal Reserve, there was a pronounced increase in business activity by February, 1925. (95) According to the Federal Reserve, an important factor in the business recovery was the large number of loans made to the Europeans which was facilitated by easy money conditions. By March, 1925, a noticeable export of gold was occurring with net gold exports of $17.8 million by the end of the year. The Federal Reserve also reported an increase in the demand for credit due both to an increase in the volume of security loans and to seasonal requirements. By December, 1925, reserve bank credit was $215 million greater than a year earlier. The Federal Reserve stated that the seasonal needs and gold exports influenced their policies that year. (96) While some government securities were sold in January, the sales stopped by February. While the discount rate had been raised in February from 3% to 3 1/2% at the New York Federal Reserve Bank, other Federal Reserve Banks ranged from 3 1/2% to 4%, and were allowed to remain at that level. Justifying its easy money policy decision, the Federal Reserve said:

"In the absence of evidence of a speculative attitude among the commercial users of credit, the Reserve System was unwilling, for the purpose of exercising a measure of restraint upon those who were borrowing in order to carry or deal in securities, to raise the discount rate at New York, and thus to exert its influence in the direction of a further increase in the cost of credit to commerce and industry at the time of the seasonal peak in the volume of commercial borrowing and in the demand for the credit to finance the marketing and export of agricultural products." (97)

Furthermore, the Federal Reserve Board justified the decision by stating that since the New York money market is the American contact point with foreign markets, raising the discount rate would attract more gold inflows which would hurt the banking situation.

The Federal Reserve had defended a policy of easy money in the interests of promoting business and in preventing future gold inflows. While recognizing the increase in security speculation, the Federal Reserve defended easy money by saying that they would not provide easy money if the speculators were commercial users of credit. Here, the Federal Reserve System apparently did not condone the instant credit expansion and independence of the system that gold inflows permitted. They also were acting to sterilize the gold exports through their easy money policy.

Overall, bankers and industrialists continued to be somewhat divided on Federal Reserve policy with many bankers supporting tight monetary policies and many industrialists supporting easy money. (98)

Strong support for the Federal Reserve System came from the Secretary of the Treasury, Andrew Mellon. In an article published in May, 1925, Mellon applauded the work of the Reserve System. (99) Mellon felt, as did others of that time period, that the current prosperity could be attributed to the Federal Reserve. Mellon stated:

"During their brief existence the Federal Reserve Banks have demonstrated beyond any doubt their value to the country... In spite of the great upheaval in the economic relations of the entire world, business in America has been able to readjust itself and continue in the line of orderly growth... That this is true may be attributed in a large degree to the operation of the Federal Reserve System." (100)

Mellon further stated that the most valuable function of the system was that of credit policy which would prolong prosperity and reduce recessions. He recommended that more state banks join the System and benefit from it, particularly during periods of emergency.

Another supporter at that time was the economist John R. Commons. He published an article in March, 1925, commending the Federal Reserve for their sterilization of gold flows policy, referring to it as an "admirable feat" in preventing the inflation of gold prices. (101) Commons felt that the Federal Reserve needed to influence both the price and the supply of credit. He commented on the dangers of bank independence from the system due to gold inflows by saying that this could create booms and collapses. Commons felt that if and when the world returned to an international gold standard the Federal Reserve System alone would protect the volume of credit and prices. Therefore, Commons approved of both the Federal Reserve's credit policy tools and sterilization of gold flows.

Clearly, not all academicians felt this way. Professors Reed and Beckhardt criticized the Federal Reserve for promoting European interests above American interests, for fueling stock speculation with easy money policies, and for being politically motivated. (102) Also supporting this opinion was W. O. Weyforth of John Hopkins University. He expressed fears that the easy money of the 1920's could cause great economic problems. Regarding the general credit situation, in 1925 Weyforth stated:

"There is much uncertainty concerning the future of currency and credit conditions in this country. To many students of banking the situation has presented elements of danger because of the possibility of overextension and the encouragement thereby given to the inflation of prices and the over-expansion of business, leading eventually to the severe crises and depression that usually follow such periods of excessive activity." (103)

According to Weyforth, the unrelenting gold flows of September, 1920-1924, furnished the basis of the over extension of credit. This, as we have already seen from the Federal Reserve Bulletin, is indeed the case. Weyforth cites Dr. B. M. Anderson, in the " Annual Report of the Secretary of the Treasury" as well as the "Chase Economic Bulletin" as supporting his contention that credit had already been expanded to a dangerous level. Gold exports, Weyfoth stated, could relieve the situation. As discussed earlier, monetary policies promoting easy money would not allow for the natural contraction once exports were established and credit expansions would continue.

Overall, while the economy appeared to prosper, security speculation, credit expansion, and the Federal Reserve's policies definitely had their critics. Some of the critics even warned of the possibility of a depression if credit expansion was not reversed. Certainly, both the advocates and critics of the System had become more vocal since a year earlier.

5. GENERAL ECONOMIC CONDITIONS (1926)

The year 1926 was marked by a recession in the housing industry with a decline in the construction of new dwelling units of

(88,000 to 849,000). (104) However, automobile registrations continued to climb and reached 19,220,885, or an increase of 1.78 million. (105) Prices declined somewhat during the year and there was rapid consolidation of business. Also, the warning signs of a heat up in stock market activity had become apparent.

The beginning of February brought expectations for further stock market acceleration and a feeling that the prosperity of 1925 came without undue strain on the economy. Recognition was given, however, to excess real estate speculation as well as to excess stock market activity. E. V. Jaeger in "When Will Stocks Reach Peak?" advised readers that before the bull market would end, more excess speculation would occur and that these excesses would cause the end of the bull market through a tightening of credit restrictions. (106) This tightening was expected to occur rapidly. Jaeger did not expect either the building or the automobile industries to continue as they had, and he was right regarding the building industry.

In March, B. C. Forbes predicted that "No, there is nothing present within our sight to warrant a pessimistic view of this country's outlook." (107) He based this on twenty five factors which included the following: well maintained security prices, high employment, a good business pace, easy money, low cost of living, lower taxes, less real estate speculation, a settled coal strike, active construction and automobile industries, more rubber, less oil price cutting, good steel production, healthy railway earnings, better than expected grain and cotton performance, inventory ordering by business, rapid utility and industry expansion, healthy sugar and animal markets, large foreign trade, a calm acceptance of large broker loans ($3.5 billion), high savings deposits, life insurance growth, and a continued optimistic outlook. Finally, an increase in the imports of luxury goods and delicacies as well as travel abroad were thought to be supportive of worldwide business stability. That this might actually mean changes in demand due to an increase in the percent of income in the hands of fewer, and wealthier, persons was not understood.

Even B. C. Forbes, who later would warn against stock market excess, had faith in the security buildup in the first half of 1926. The beginning of 1926 brought a wild bidding up of selected securities. Coca Cola went from a low of $80 in 1925 to a high of $178 in 1926. Forbes informed his readers in March, 1926, to pay little attention to these developments. (108) It was the reasoning of the time that these developments would not effect prospects of business conditions, as an end to the bull market was expected by the end of 1926. This feeling continued in May, when Forbes reported that with output, employment, and consumption high, a recession would not occur. (109) The expansion of installment credit was thought soon to be ended by public warnings, and the stabilization of Europe seemed imminent. The fact that brokers' loans had taken a temporary dip, and that the New York Reserve Bank discount rate had been slashed to 3 1/2% increased confidence in the availability of easy money.

Finally, in August, 1926, Forbes printed an article, "Has Stock Speculation Become Dangerous?", which attested to the dangers of this type of speculation. (110) While two thirds of the February - March 30 point drop had been recovered, Forbes felt that speculation in certain industrial issues had been carried dangerously far. The source of this speculation was the stock market pool in which groups of investors selected popular stocks and then manipulated their prices up. Forbes warned against purchasing these stocks with the bull gamblers, and said that if the practice continued the Federal Reserve would almost certainly raise the discount rate at New York to 4%. On September 15, 1926, the editor of Forbes Magazine advised would be investors that speculation in the stock market had become dangerous. (111) Further, he stated that the upturn in generous business had bolstered the speculation.

At the end of 1926 the following developments were noted in the economy:

(1)   A slowing down in chain store and mail order sales;

(2)   A sharp decline in construction as well as a moderate decline in steel;

(3)   A slight decline in employment;

(4)   Lower than expected money rates;

(5)   Gains in railway earnings;

(6)   Declines in the prices of agricultural commodities and irregular prices in metals, rubber, and oil production; and,

(7)   A slight decrease in the amount of brokers loans. (112)

6. FEDERAL RESERVE POLICY (1926)

According to the "Thirteenth Annual Report" of the Federal Reserve Board, 1926 was characterized by healthy business activity, increased savings going into investment, increased bank credit, easy money rates, and favorable conditions in short term money. The prices of commodities declined 6% over the year, and a great amount of this decline was in agricultural products. Overall, the discount rates were maintained at 4% except for a reduction to 3 1/2% in New York City, and open market investments were maintained with small fluctuations at the same rate as a year earlier. This was due to a year of stable conditions according to their report.

The Federal Reserve also commented on bank suspensions. The 956 bank suspensions, mainly in agricultural states, were cited in the annual report as being mostly nonmember banks, (796 out of the total of 956). In analyzing the reasons for these failures, the Federal Reserve cited an excess of banks, poor management, and insufficient capital. The move to urban areas and unsound loans to farmers were also cited as causes. However, most interesting in this analysis was the Federal Reserve's note of the beginning of a bank run panic. As is now known, at that time the Federal Reserve did not tie nonmember bank problems to being a possible future cause of difficulties resulting in runs of member banks. Apparently, they were aware in a general sense of the results of panic in 1926:

"A contributory cause of bank suspensions has been the fact that with frequent suspensions of banks in the same neighborhood the confidence of depositors has been shaken and they have withdrawn their money from the banks. This withdrawal of deposits has accentuated the weakness of the situation and in some cases has been a factor in causing additional suspensions of banks which might otherwise have been able to continue in operation." (113)

The attitude of reviewers of Federal Reserve Policy as it had been implemented so far was mixed. As a group, bankers blamed the Federal Reserve for speculation. By 1926, bankers also believed that the lack of restraining credit had caused the market rapidly to accelerate. Industrialists naturally countered in favor of easy money and permanent prosperity. (114)

Henry Chandler, an economist, was careful to delineate the difficult issues facing the Federal Reserve. (115) On the one hand he noted that European recovery depended upon further Federal Reserve support in making American funds easy to obtain. Also facing the Federal Reserve, Chandler noted, was the necessary control of the speculative situation. Recognizing the criticism that the Federal Reserve faced, he asserted the inherent difficulty in determining when domestic versus foreign factors should be decisive in credit policy and vice versa. No set rules existed to resolve this dilemma, but Chandler felt that so far the Federal Reserve's stabilization efforts had been rewarding. The conservative attitudes of bankers, and Chandler also included businessmen, were needed to place sufficient pressure on the Federal Reserve to insure that domestic interests against speculation were promoted. Yet he also implied that European programs must be completed.

An interesting analysis of Federal Reserve policy from 1921 - 1926 was given by another economist, H. L. Reed of Cornell University. Reed stated that the Federal Reserve Board faced many problems politically. (116) Congress attempted to pass a bill that would not permit the Federal Reserve banks to raise the discount rate above 2% without the permission of Congress. Since the Board could only review rates set by the various districts, it was limited in its power. It could, however, remove these district's directors, but this drastic step was usually avoided. As far as open market purchases were concerned, an Open Market Committee was formed to harmonize the operations of the various Federal Reserve banks. In the latter half of 1924, the Federal Reserve relaxed credit as a reaction to the recession of 1923-1924. Reed felt that this open market purchase policy was questionable. The Federal Reserve Board had explained that the purchases were made so that later security sales would force reserve bank credit under the discount rate influence. However, Reed felt that member banks could increase credit without rediscounting, and that the policy was futile. Reed felt the policy was dangerous as the money would have to go somewhere and the Board had replied unofficially that it could be poured into the securities market, which outraged Reed. Reed commented:

"If this were the thought of the Reserve administration, it is our desire to attack it vigorously. We do not believe that the securities market can be regarded as an independent reservoir into which a large volume of funds can conveniently be poured without incurring the danger of weakening the general financial structure... The New York promotion profession is normally capable of devising all sorts of new offerings for distribution to the rest of the country, provided the funds seem available. Easy money is tremendously important in encouraging such activities. In other words, it appears that the policy of the Reserve Banks in these months was to assist Wall Street in rigging the market for a campaign of distribution." (117)

Reed continued that he felt that the real motives of the Federal Reserve Board were to make dividend and expense payments and to make good earnings. However, he added that because of the outflow of gold expected in 1925 (which did actually occur) there was no reason to saturate the market with cheap money.

Reed concluded that economists instantly must criticize future actions of the Federal Reserve which are not perceived to be in the spirit of their 1923 policy statement, and that economists both demand that the Board fully explain their actions and insist that better qualified men sit on the Board.

At the time he was serving as an Assistant Federal Reserve Agent at the Federal Reserve Bank in New York, Randolph Burgess described the impact of the Reserve Banks on the New York money market in April, 1926. (118) In describing the system, Burgess nonjudgmentally points out that the ability to borrow from the Reserve Banks provided a mechanism for rapid expansion in the New York money market, even though such funds were technically only to be acquired for emergencies or for seasonal requirements. The mechanism, he asserted, would also be available to restrain overzealous expansion.

Governor Strong of the Federal Reserve Bank of New York, a man who later would promote foreign loan interests over American speculative concerns and permit credit expansion to over fuel the stock market, discussed in May, 1926, the benefits of the use of open market operations:

"The influence that the Reserve System exercises in the money market may be described in this way. If speculation, rise in prices and possibly other considerations that would move the Reserve Banks to tighten up a bit on their use of credit come...and we have a large amount of government securities...it is a more effective program, we find by actual experience, to begin to sell our government securities. It lays a foundation for an advance in our discount rate. If the reverse conditions appear, then the purchase of securities eases the money market and permits the reduction of our discount rate. This is a big country, a vast organization, and I feel that we have still much to learn about how those things should be done. So far as we have gone in our experience and under world conditions as they are, it seems to me that the foundation for rate changes can be more safely and better made by those operations in the open market than would be possible otherwise, and the effect is less dramatic and less alarming to the country if it is done in that way than if we just make advances and reductions in our discount rate." (119)

Finally, J. G. Donley, a business writer in Forbes Magazine, warned that the Federal Reserve should not allow for further exhorbitant increases in credit. (120) Donley pointed to the fact that stock and bond loans had grown by $341 million over the year. (Total loans and discounts had increased by $600 million.) Donley was surprised that the Federal Reserve had not tightened money rates.

While bankers feared credit expansion and industrialists applauded it, business writers saw nothing to fear in the speculative activity until the second half of the year.They were aware before that time of the impending slowdown in construction activity, and they did voice loud warnings toward the end of the year concerning the bull market. Actually, an end to the bull market was expected by business writers by the end of the year with price declines in manipulated stocks. This attested to the fact that business writers not only were aware of overbidding but felt that the end would come much sooner (three years, in fact) than it actually did. Their expectations that the Federal Reserve would facilitate a tightening of credit, however, were ill-founded.

The Federal Reserve saw nothing to fear in 1926, but rather reported it as a year of healthy conditions and easy money. The nasty issue of nonmember rural bank failures was addressed and dismissed as largely a result of bad management and an oversupply of banks. Bank panics were also recognized as playing an important role in these failures, but no connection was drawn by the Federal Reserve Bank between these runs and later runs on member banks.

Critics of Federal Reserve policy gave mixed reviews. On the one hand, the tools of open market operations and credit expansion for the New York money market were applauded. On the other hand, H. L. Reed chastised the Federal Reserve for dumping credit into the speculative arena in order to assert control over member banks. Reed was also critical of the credentials of those on the Board. Probably the best analysis of the dilemma of the time was Chandler's description of the conflicting goal of restraining speculative credit versus providing easy money in order to further European stability. An inadequate resolution of this problem and a favoring by the Board of European interests would, in 1927, create the easy money that would be cited later as the point of no return for Wall Street.

7. GENERAL ECONOMIC CONDITIONS (1927)

The year 1927 was a recessionary year with difficulties apparent in some of the major industries. The agricultural sector was still suffering. Residential construction slipped by 39,000 units to 810,000. (120) Other industries showed continuing strength, such as the increase of 1.8 million automobile registrations (to 19,220,885). (121) Speculative activity was very rapid, and the top 1% to 5% of income brackets were receiving greater disproportionate shares of the national income. Initially, the recessionary conditions had led to a somewhat more restrained monetary policy and the growth of the money supply declined. However, as the recession continued and as the pressure to support European markets increased, the Federal Reserve eased monetary policy in large part to accommodate Great Britain, France, and Germany. *It is believed today that the easy money policies of 1927 sealed the fate of this country and steered the course to the Great Depression.*

While prosperity was still felt to be evident by many, writers in Forbes Magazine were aware of the fundamental economic weaknesses and of the dangers of speculative fever. B. C. Forbes had not changed his position of foreboding of earlier years. In April, 1927, Forbes was fairly optimistic, predicting that in spite of the upswing in commercial failures and other uncertainties, the future should be approached hopefully. (122) By June, 1927, Forbes pronounced "I am beginning to be afraid of the stock market." (123) He stated that record breaking heights attained in the securities market were the result of professional manipulation and could not possibly be indicative of real business conditions. He noted that easy money was the facilitation of the bidding, and that easy money alone was not enough to hold up the market. Business profits would have to move up into the realm of the record breaking stock price quotations in order for real stability to set in. Forbes did not feel that business would pick up sufficiently to warrant this because of the recessions in the building and steel industries, as well as in other areas. Prices had declined and Forbes feared that the stock market would interfere with business conditions.

By early November, stocks indeed had fallen (from an average of $50 to $20 per share). In "Business and Stocks Move Very Unevenly", Forbes stated that such developments should have been obvious as the business pace did not warrant the securities price rise. (124) With key sectors of industry depressed, some of the bulls were becoming bears. Forbes believed that agriculture was bound to improve as cotton had. Money was still cheap, so Forbes felt that the downturn was predicated upon corporate reports which revealed diminished earnings.

Another writer, R. W. Mc Neel warned readers against the folly of current beliefs that business cycles were gone. (125) The current wave of prosperity had run beyond its course according to Mc Neel. The fact that stocks were being avidly purchased at prices above those justified by income return or earnings attested to Mc Neel's belief that the financial world had accepted the theory that business cycles were a thing of the past. Well defined business cycles were the norm all over, and he felt that their very persistency should warn against believing in permanent prosperity. Mc Neel did not believe that the Federal Reserve could prevent the periodic recurrence of depressions and recessions. He did believe, however, that they could do much to improve things.

Mc Neel felt that the wave of prosperity could be accounted for by the presence of certain abnormal factors. These included post war construction, abnormally high demand due to increased wages, abnormal buying in large quantities due to installment credit, and abnormally low prices of finished goods depressing business buying. Because of the fear of a continued price recession, businesses were afraid to buy ahead in case prices would slip further. According to Mc Neel, this lack of business buying had been misinterpreted as prudence in not overproducing. Excessive borrowing to purchase more stock was perceived by Mc Neel as dangerous. He felt that price deflation was not due so much to technological advances as to working back from wartime to peacetime prices. Furthermore, consumption demand was not keeping pace with production, preventing future ordering and the normal expansion of business. Such demand changes were discussed in CHAPTER I and attributed to the rapid absorption of income gains by the upper classes who did not have the average demand per capita for basic goods and services.

Readers of the day did receive sound warnings based on logical conclusions of the needed relationship between business profits and security values. Belief in the elimination of business cycles had been accepted by many, and was set out as a very dangerous assumption. Changed demand, presumably due to a redistribution of income to the upper classes, and hesitancy on the part of business had been recognized and coined as "abnormal".

8. FEDERAL RESERVE POLICY (1927)

The Federal Reserve judged 1927 to be a year of high productivity with a gradual recession from July through December. (126) By the end of the year commodity prices had slipped slightly. The decrease in construction was noteable in both residential and industrial construction. The Federal Reserve System noted that while demand for loans to finance current business operations did not increase, total loans and investments increased by $2.8 billion for member banks, of which $1.7 billion was in urban areas. Commercial loans actually declined while acceptances and broker loans dramatically increased. Noting the financing of brokers loans by business, the Federal Reserve said:

"Increased supply of funds in the hands of corporations, owing in part to the somewhat reduced volume of industrial and commercial activity, in part to the growth in volume of industrial and commercial activity, and in part to the growth in the volume of funds which they have obtained through security issues, has been an important factor increasing so-called brokers loans on account of others." (127)

Gold imports during the first half of 1927 again permitted member banks to liquidate loans at Reserve Banks. The discount rate was left alone and there were no open market operations. In May,

1927, as gold was exported, the Reserve Banks bought securities to offset (sterilize) these exports. With gold exports slackening between June and September, the Federal Reserve stated that it continued to purchase government securities in the amount of $80 million to ease credit.

"This policy was adopted by the System in consideration of the recession in business in the United States, of the relatively heavy indebtedness of member banks, and of the tendency towards firmer conditions in the money market. During this period it also became evident that there was a serious credit stringency in European countries generally, and it was felt that easy money in this country would help foreign countries to meet their autumn demand for credit and exchange without unduly depressing their exchanges or increasing the cost of credit to trade and industry. Easier credit conditions abroad would also facilitate the financing of our exports and would thus be of benefit to American producers. By purchasing securities at that time the Federal Reserve banks were in fact successful in easing the condition of the money market and in exerting a favorable influence on the international financial situation." (128)

The Federal Reserve Board was pleased to see the discount rate slip from 4% to 3 1/2% at all member banks. They were sufficiently sure of their action in easing money rates to openly supply the reasons for it.

From September 1, 1927 to January 1, 1928, this nation's gold stock decreased by $209 million. The Federal Reserve Board offset this by open market purchases until November, but the Board allowed the withdrawls to exert their contractionary influence on credit after November, 1927.

"To summarize, reserve bank policy in the early part of the year, when gold imports were exerting an influence toward easier money, was to refrain from taking an active position toward the market; in the spring and summer, in the absence of considerable net gold movements, the system's policy was expressed in easing the money market through the purchase of securities and the reduction of discount rates; in early autumn, when an outward movement of gold began, the system offset in part the effects of gold withdrawls through purchases in the open market, and finally in the closing months of the year the system policy, in view of the rapid expansion of member bank credit, was to permit the continued outflow of gold to exert its customary tightening influence on credit conditions." (129)

Therefore, not until the end of 1927 was the policy of sterilization of gold flows reversed.

Opinion regarding the Federal Reserve System was again somewhat mixed. Aside from business writers in Forbes Magazine, the tenor in 1927 was somewhat positive. Speaking in general support of the Federal Reserve System, Allyn A. Young of Harvard University stated that the System had been wisely planned. (130) Allowing that the degree to which the the system had actually contributed to stability was questionable, he supported their policy mechanisms and cautioned against forcing them to rely upon specific rules of decision making. Young felt that the wisdom and judgment of the board were more important than the facts, and that the Board was developing a sound decision making basis.

John R. Commons of the University of Wisconsin stated that the Federal Reserve was a necessary economic and legal power. In April, 1927, Commons recommended that in order to reverse the deflation of prices accompanying the recession, the discount rate should be lowered and government securities purchased. (131) Commons spoke in favor of easing the money supply, which was done, and which later would lead to disasterous results.

Also speaking in support of the System was business writer Meryle Stanley Rukeyser. In January, 1927, Rukeyser praised the Federl Reserve System for allowing gold to be exported to Europe. (132) He felt that a large part of the reasoning for Europe's return to the gold standard was an effort to please the United States so that the Federal Reserve Board would continue to make loans easy to get. According to Rukeyser, Benjamin Strong of the Federal Reserve and M. Norman, Governor of the Bank of England, were the chief architects of the plan. He felt that how the ouflow would effect American prosperity would depend upon the policy of the Federal Reserve. Rukeyser thought that sterilizing gold inflows was a wise move on the part of the Federal Reserve as it prevented gold inflation. Rukeyser's opinion was that security market speculation was the fault of the gold inflows, not of the Federal Reserve.

In 1927, a cautious but supportive Randolph Burgess of the New York Federal Reserve Bank analyzed the results of Federal

Reserve credit policy. (133) Burgess felt that it would take at least twenty years to really understand the implications of their actions.

"It would be difficult to find another example of easy money bulwarked by such a large mass of reserves, which offers stability and a guarantee of some continuance of stability. The unusual nature of the economic circumstances of the past few years makes one cautious in making any claims with regard to what the Federal Reserve System has done for the stability of business."

Burgess further observed that the Federal Reserve had removed much of the seasonal fluctuation of intrest rates, and that since the institution of credit policy, prosperity had followed. The theory that they were there to reduce the normal business cycles was demonstrated by their use of tools (especially the open market operations) to tighten and ease credit as they felt necessary. Most importantly, Burgess pointed to the Federal Reserve's actions under the leadership of Governor Strong to ease credit so that Europe could return to the gold standard. Burgess concluded that while caution in evaluating the Federal Reserve was necessary, they had appeared to promote business stability.

While referring to the Federal Reserve System as an admirable performer on the whole, Paul Warburg of the Federal Reserve criticised the Reserve for not lessening unemployed funds in the New York Stock Exchange. Warburg stated:

"While the Reserve System is not directly connected with, nor responsible for, the operations of the stock exchange, it could not be unaffected by a tottering of this Colossus that keeps on growing from year to year. For if disaster should overcome the exchange, the banks would be involved and the banks are the wards of the Reserve System." (135)

Warburg recommended a system of term settlements in order to cool the overheated market. This would enable a gradual withdrawl of funds from the market. While extolling the virtues of open market operations, he stressed that enough securities needed to be available to buy and sell in order to make a difference. This, as we saw earlier, was a problem that the system would have faced had they started the sale of securities earlier as only a limited amount were in circulation. Warburg supported the concept of a high-powered Federal Reserve stating that the Reserve System needed both power and the will to assert such power.

Overall, support for the Federal Reserve was fairly impressive even though business writers feared for the future safety of the nation. Shortly after the stock market crash of 1929, Dr. Harold. H. Reed evaluated Federal Reserve policy. A summary of his opinions regarding the period 1924-1927 is in order before moving on to an analysis of 1928. (136)

With weak foreign markets prevailing, Reed felt that it was not difficult to perceive of the intentions of the Federal Reserve in easing the money supply. The increased demand for American products by Europeans and the need to restore their economies was very real. Reed pointed to the fact that many economists of the time not only felt that the discount rate reductions were necessary, but that they should have been made earlier. Reed stated that critics immediately siezed upon the subservience of American investors to foreign investors. The rate reductions apparently had been delayed until this point for this reason as well as fears of fueling further speculation. He felt that by looking back from the perspective of 1930, it was easy to criticize the lack of restraining measures imposed by the Federal Reserve. By August, 1927, it seemed that the Federal Reserve should have been able to question the wisdom of their rate reductions. However, the complex issues of the time, particularly the European situation, made their actions understandable at least until August, 1927.

From 1924-1927, three major problems emerged: the switch from rural/agricultural credit to urban/financial credit, the overbuilding of the general credit structure, and liquidity impairments. Reed asserted that responsibility for this had to be placed on the Federal Reserve in that they had not provided help that would trickle down into the rural areas, and that they had made street loans attractive. It was not the Federal Reserve's fault that member banks had aggravated the situation by reclassifying loans so as to draw down reserve requirements.

The decisions facing the Federal Reserve were complex and political. Perhaps the Federal Reserve had become so wrapped up in the gravity of their decisions that they could not grasp clearly the danger of the stock market situation as business writers of the time had. Staffed by political appointees who were not necesarily banking experts, they must have been particularly succeptable to political pressures brought upon them. The support of economists such as those discussed here must have lent weighty support to the strength of their convictions. While understandable to a degree, the folly of their decisions is inescapable and it gives credence to the proposition that a more careful and independent month to month review of the facts would have led to an earlier tightening of the money market.

9. GENERAL ECONOMIC CONDITIONS (1928)

The year 1928 brought a continuing decline in residential construction and a decrease in the number of newly registered vehicles. New dwelling units dropped approximately 57,000 to 735,000, and automobile registrations dropped approximately 800,000 to 21,308,507. (137)   Security values were now way out of line with industry performance, and the Federal Reserve finally acted to put the brakes on the booming stock market.   Attempts to constrain the money supply through raising the discount rate to 5%, and through purchasing government securities would now prove futile in curtailing speculation. *The stock market was beyond control. The Federal Reserve constraints merely served to put the damper on productive business investments.* An income tax reduction, which is contrary to policies of spending restraint, occurred in 1928.   Finally, basic industries other than those mentioned above such as agriculture were still in trouble, and the upper income brackets continued to receive disproportionately increasing percentages of national income.

Not realizing how late in the game restraint had come, writers of the day felt that these changes would change the situation.   In February, 1928, B. C. Forbes wrote an article entitled, "B. C. Forbes Sees Betterment in Business" in which he applauded the rise in the discount rate and concluded that the business outlook was improved. (138)   While the agriculture outlook was dim, Forbes stated that United States Steel and other large companies were expecting a better return on investment than in 1927.   The key problem cited was potential overproduction which could repress business recovery. Forbes concluded by advising the reader to stay away from speculation in the big bull stocks and to invest in oil and utilities.

R. W. Schabacker, also writing in Forbes Magazine, stated on March 1, 1928, that the increase in the discount rate, then at 4%, had not hurt any industries, but that it should act to curb speculation. Schabacker, like many others, did not realize how far out of control

the situation really was. (139) In May, 1928, Forbes expressed his fear of the speculative mania that seemed to continue with unlimited credit and aggressive trading. (140) He cited a large public following and cheap money as the factors feeding the speculation. He correctly expected that the discount rate would be advanced barring any significant signs of improvement. Banker's acceptances were at unprecedented heights and rates for both these and brokers' loans were undergoing rapid acceleration. Forbes concluded:
"Either the stock market will act more rationally or the Federal Reserve authorities at New York, Washington, and elsewhere will take more vigorous action." (141)

By June, 1928, Forbes was of the opinion, not widely held in speculative circles, that high stocks would crash and that by November 6, 1928, many stocks would be available at low prices. (142) He attributed this to the advance of call money from 6% to 6 1/2%, time money from 4 1/2% to 5 1/2%, and the selling of government securities by the Federal Reserve. Member banks were tapping the Federal Reserve Banks heavily, and gold outflows to foreign countries were substantial. Forbes found ridiculous the claims of some businessmen that even if stock prices were not merited now, future strong business activity would support them. Unemployment and a lower movement of goods did not warrant the speculative enthusiasm.

Summing up the factors favoring improvement, in September, 1928, Forbes cited nine. (143) These were good harvest factors, level prices, low unemployment, high motor transportation, building activity, automobile and steel industry success, retail trade gains, and a good business sentiment. On the negative side, Forbes cited a weak money market and the uncertainties associated with presidential elections. As far as the money market was concerned, gold exports of $600 million removed the basis for billions in credit. With stock prices and brokers' loans even higher, the Federal Reserve had been unable to end the speculation. Bootleg lending from outsiders with idle funds pushed loans up another $2 billion, and call and time loans as well as bankers acceptances and commercial paper were reaching all time rates. Manipulated stocks continued to soar. Non-manipulated stock activity was passive. Forbes felt that stock prices would fall by November, but that the election could introduce new speculation impetus.

Concluding, until approximately May, 1928, business writers were encouraged by the potential of restricted credit. After the first four months of 1928, it became apparent that speculative fever had not ended and a crash (not of the magnitude of The Great Crash) was expected in 1928. Those factors given as encouraging for business recovery were in fact not as encouraging as presented. The agriculture sector was in real trouble, wholesale prices were teetering on the edge of collapse, building activity had fallen off, and the rate of increase in automobile registration had fallen off. The negative factors, particularly the Federal Reserve's inability to cool off the heat of speculation, were more accurate and more telling of the grim story ahead.

10. FEDERAL RESERVE POLICY (1928)

According to the Federal Reserve:
"In the autumn of 1927 the Federal Reserve System, in view of business recession in this country and a money stringency abroad, adopted a policy directed towards easier money." (144)

This was during a gold outflow (which would decrease the country's gold supply by $231 million by the year's end) which was permitted in late 1927 to exert its contractionary effect. This gold outflow was offset in 1928 by open market operations which were discontinued towards the end of 1928. Credit was easy to obtain from January to June, 1928. In late June the discount rate was raised from 4% to 4 1/2% at all Federal Reserve Banks. From May to July, 1928, commercial loans increased slightly and security loans decreased. In August, 1928, the situation turned around. Commercial credit declined, stock exchange activity grew, and the volume of bank credit grew. The Federal Reserve stated:

"Because the System has a broad responsibility for the general soundness of credit conditions, and because growth of bank credit for any purpose ultimately leads to a demand for reserve bank credit, it is its duty to use its influence against undue credit expansion in any direction. (145)

The Federal Reserve pointed out that the greatest bank credit expansion was in securities. From 1925-1928, security loans advanced from $6.7 billion to $9.1 billion, and bank holdings of investments increased from $8.9 billion to $10.8 billion. In defending their actions, the Federal reserve said:

"In determining upon credit policy the Federal Reserve System is always under the necessity of balancing the advantages and disadvantages that are likely to follow a given course of action. Low money rates may have a favorable effect on domestic business, but at the same time may stimulate speculation in securities, commodities, or real estate. High money rates, on the other hand, may exert a moderating influence on speculation, but at the same time may result in a higher cost of credit to all lines of business, and thus be detrimental to commerce and industry. Ultimately, they may draw gold from abroad, which would tend to ease the domestic situation." (146)

According to "Executive Opinion", statements such as these came because the Federal Reserve was getting dual advice. (147) Some pressured the Board that tightened credit would be deleterious to the international economy. Others argued that easy money had encouraged excess speculation. When the Federal Reserve finally tightened up monetary policy in 1928, it was too late and the stock market took no notice.

Evaluation of Federal reserve policy was still diverse. The Honorable Roy. A. Young, Governor of the Federal Reserve Board, Washington, D. C. spoke in support of the Federal Reserve System. He stated that a much larger credit structure was built on a smaller stockpile of gold than in 1927 because member banks had increased borrowings by $500 million from the Federal Reserve. He felt that this meant that the System was operating as intended. He said that there were many people who were more concerned about an unsound credit structure than the Federal Reserve. However, he believed that any instabilities would be self-correcting and that those who would lose some money during a period of correction could only blame themselves. Young criticized those who were dissatisfied with the unpredictability of the Federal Reserve. Young asserted that conditions determined appropriate Federal Reserve policy, not vice versa. It is not surprising that in view of the earlier discussed disputes between the Federal Reserve Board and the Federal Reserve Bank of New York over constraining credit, the Board found its most avid Bank supporters in Washington and not in New York.

Taking the other side of the issue was O. M. W. Sprague of the Harvard Business School. On April 20, 1928, Sprague published an article blaming the Reserve Banks for the inflation of brokers' loans. He felt that many of the speculators were relying upon the Federal Reserve to protect the market from collapse because the Federal Reserve had taken credit publicly for policies leading to stability. Restraint had been abandoned by those who relied upon the Federal Reserve. The future would bring either a relatively passive policy of restraint by raising discount rates or a more active one of open market operations in order to raise the cost of call money immediately. Sprague thought that this action, had it been taken earlier, along with the raising of the discount rate, would have broken the bull market without substantial injury. However, recognizing the point to which things had arrived, Sprague warned:

"Whatever the adoption of drastic measures would now precipitate, a spectacular collapse in the security markets is by no means certain. But were it to have that result, the consequences might well prove far less damaging than those which may be anticipated if the market continues in its present mood until it collapses from its own weakness and excess." (149)

The Federal Reserve Board had moved too slowly to tighten credit conditions and while some support for their lack of action could be found within their own System, the New York Reserve Bank, located in the center of speculative action, opposed them. Alert and well informed economists such as Sprague were aware of the terrible dangers of putting the brakes on too fast now that it was too late. If the 1927 easy money conditions can be blamed for the most awesome fueling of the speculative activity, 1928 was the year in which the Federal Reserve bypassed its last option for effective, restraining action. What was to ensue would demonstrate the lack of wisdom in resorting to judgmental evaluations of conditions, without hard and proven policy guidelines.

One last comment must be made before proceeding to an evaluation of 1929. Benjamin Strong, formerly mentioned here as the chief architect in promoting easy money policy to aid Europe, died in 1928, too soon to see the ill-fated results of his actions. In a resolution at the Tenth Annual Dinner of the American Acceptance Council, grateful words were spoken for his efforts:

"The members of the Acceptance Council owe Governor Strong a particular debt of gratitude for the courage and breadth of view with which he approached the momentous problems of open market operations and international relations.. It is safe to say that he is entitled to the fullest recognition for having acted as the pathfinder and pioneer in establishing close relations with other central banks together into an intimate group united in an effort to assist other countries in their struggles to restore fiscal order and exchange stability." (150)

11. GENERAL ECONOMIC CONDITIONS (1929)

A review of the facts regarding conditions in 1929 depicts a tumultuous year, culminating in the October stock market crash, and followed by a series of denials concerning the severity of the crash's impact upon the future of the economy.

Over the course of 1929, automobile registrations rose at a slower rate, 1.75 million, to a total of 23,060,421. Residential construction continued its dramatic decline. Only 509,000 units were built that year, a decline of 244,000 from 1928. (151) By 1929, the business consolidations that had been occurring over the decade had resulted in 47% of corporate wealth and 38% of business wealth. Approximately 22% of the nation's wealth was in the control of a mere 200 corporations. (152) Wholesale prices were beginning to fall. The per capita farm income was $477 beneath the national average, or $273 versus $750. (153) By 1929, corporations were providing the major source of speculative funds. (154) Common stock prices were 128% above 1926 levels. (155) Foreign investment had peaked at an all time high of $17 billion. (156) Commercial loans were now only 45% of total loans. (157) Federal Reserve policy continued to tighten with a long sought, but too late rise in the discount rate to 6% in August, 1929. (158) Action to slow the wheels of speculation before tragedy would strike was now a lost alternative. *On October 23 and 24, 1929, the stock market crashed.* (159) Following the crash, the Federal Reserve eased the money supply by making open market purchases and by reducing the discount rate.

By September, business writers admitted that the weather was "...Fair but Cooler" for business. (160) While employment was up and corporations held surplus cash and large dividends, certain lows were evident. (Surplus cash was viewed positively.) Among these lows, business was not keeping up a productive pace, prices and retail trade lagged, the agriculture industry was suffering, and stock prices were above industry earning expectations. Late in September, business was viewed as being in an unhealthy state. (161) With credit constricted and a lower than normal rate of business expansion, the business outlook was poor. The great number of security loans pushed the money rates up so that new credit and healthy business expansion were impossible. In *Business Week*, October 5, 1929, business conditions were labelled unsafe. (162) The stock market chill was thought to be a normal settling process and not the beginning of a collapse. In spite of favored optimism, brokers' loans were being investigated. In early October, 1929, at the American Bankers Association Convention an unofficial investigation of brokers' loans was demanded. (163) The retiring President, Craig Hazelwood, stated that the movement of banks into stock market speculation was dangerous. Another article pointed out that brokers' loans had skyrocketed to $6.8 billion. (164) Credit from the Federal Reserve was going into the stock market, although overall borrowing had declined to $63 billion. The decline, however, was due to a large purchase of bills by the Federal Reserve in the amount of $59 million.

Continued hopefulness was manifest in an article in October which had canvassed the opinions of 5600 businessmen. (165) This large survey sample felt that the volume of business would climb by approximately 5%. While high interest rates prevented distributors from financing stocks, large savings withdrawals nationwide were being made to play the stock market. However:

"...general conditions throughout the country and business today are believed by most authorities to be so healthy that a prolonged recession in activity in the near future is hardly to be expected." (166)

By October 19, 1929, Wall Street reflected a general price decline interspersed with rallies. (167) The Federal Reserve's buying of bills reflected some easing of the money market. Loans and investments fell, but brokers' loans increased. New York banks invested in the call market due to the slack in commercial demand and Federal Reserve credit increased by $25 million during the week.

After the stock market crash (October 23rd through 24the) predictions for future economic strength were positive. On November 2, 1929, the business outlook was "...clearing but continued cool." (168) It was felt that as long as business authorities would not feed the hysteria, that business would return to normal. While some trade would slacken, *Business Week* writers believed that business activity would be good in 1930, that banks would weather the storm well, that brokers' loans would decline by $1 billion, that discount rates would be lower, and that interest rates on loans for productive, rather than speculative purposes would be favorable. The New York Federal Reserve bank had already reduced its rate from 6% to 5%.

In interpreting the stock market crash, an article entitled "What the Wall Street Crash Means" was printed on November 2, 1929. (169) The crash was interpreted to mean that business conditions should always determine stock market prices, that banks and investment trusts must not dominate the market, that business expansion would be slowed temporarily, and that business would have to go back to work. It was felt that money would be cheaper and that a somewhat disorderly deflation had to be expected. What it should not mean, business writers stressed, was that real wealth had diminished, that the public would no longer speculate, that there would be a depression, that stock prices overall would recede to the 1923 level, that common stocks would no longer serve as investments, or that the Federal Reserve was to blame.

By December 11, 1929, The Great Depression was referred to as "a bad case of seasonality". (170) The fears that a sour stock market meant that bad business conditions were present were considered to be an exaggeration. Much of the lack of business performance was actually thought to be due to seasonal factors and the effects of the preceding excessive expansion. Automobile production, the steel industry..., etc., were all linked to seasonality, and their respective trends were given to support this contention.

12. FEDERAL RESERVE POLICY (1929)

The beginning of 1929 showed a greater amount of Reserve bank credit outstanding than ever before. This was due to skyrocketing broker and member bank security loans. According to the Federal Reserve:

"The measures taken by the Federal Reserve Bank in the year 1928 to firm money conditions by sales of open market investments and by successive increases in discount rates from 3 1/2% to 5% had not proved adequate." (171)

By 1928 through 1929, the Federal Reserve realized that it needed to restrain the growth of security credit without hurting business.

"With the system portfolio of government securities practically exhausted by the sales made in the first half of the year, 1928, the main reliance in a further firming of money conditions must have been further marking up of Federal Reserve discount rates unless some other expedient could be brought to bear in the situation." (172)

Yet, the Federal Reserve Board, against the insistence of the New York Federal Reserve Bank, did not want to raise the discount rate. The Board stated that the economy was in good shape in February, 1929, and that in large part this economic health was due to the Federal Reserve.

The Board felt that speculative credit increases interfered with that system. In order to protect commercial loans, the Board asked its member banks not to engage in financing speculative channels. This "direct pressure" tactic was believed, according to the "Annual Report" of 1929, to have been successful "resulting in a substantial conservation of credit resources." (173) Buying rates for bills for reserve banks were raised from 4 1/2% to 5 3/8%. By spring of 1929, reserve banks began to raise the discount rates. In August, 1929, the discount rate was approximately 6%. By October, 1929, brokers' loans were funded almost entirely by nonbanking lenders. After the stock market crash, the large liquidation in loans caused the Federal Reserve to ease the money supply through open market purchases. The discount rate was then reduced to 4 1/2%.

"This reversal of policy, made possible by diminution in the demand for credit in the security markets, appeared desirable also in view of the sharp reduction in business activity." (174)

The Federal Reserve believed at this time that the decline was due largely to the security price drop, as high security prices had fuelled business.

Professor H. L.Reed, in "Federal Reserve Policy and Brokers' Loans", analyzed speculative policy on the part of the Federal Reserve in March, 1929. (175) Pointing to the growth of brokers' loans as the major problem facing the System at that time, Reed noted that such loans were depriving agriculture and commerce of needed credit. That, coupled with the notion that security prices were too high, led some to believe that a violent collapse was brewing. However, Reed disagreed with these contentions, stating that the Federal Reserve member banks could not justify curbing loans on the grounds that the stock market threatened business conditions. Only total bank credit should be affected by the Federal Reserve. The brokers' loan problem could be cured by a normal application of credit restraint on their part. Since this policy had been adopted by the Federal Reserve in 1923, Reed noted that raising or lowering of the discount rate had indeed changed credit outstanding. Reed asserted that periods of easy money (such as the easy money created in 1927 for the benefit of the Europeans) would not automatically stimulate commercial borrowing, but that security markets would increase credit utilization. He did not feel that a discriminatory rate imposed against banks with street loans would be advisable. The Reserve Banks had already hurt the situation by creating easy money in both 1924 and 1927, demonstrating their lack of ability in determining how credit should be employed. Finally, it was recommended that the Federal Reserve develop a definitive guiding policy.

On October 12, 1929, the credit situation was evaluated in "World Credit Tangle No Nearer Solution". (176) There it was stated that by attracting gold to New York, the Federal Reserve System had to extend seasonal credit to other areas of the country. Hence, borrowing in Chicago, San Francisco, and Cleveland had increased while their holdings of gold had decreased. In assistance, the Federal Reserve System bought bankers' acceptances. This caused an easing of money in New York further fueling speculation rather than assisting industry and agriculture.

"Thus when a time comes for a redistribution of the nation's gold, or when business needs dictate lower money rates, difficulties are in prospect. Either New York will be seriously discomfited by a heavy outflow of gold or it will be forced to maintain a high enough rate to prevent that action. The free and unhindered movement of gold, the basis of all credit, is a basic principal of the financial setup in the United States, and essential to business. The elements of an unpleasant situation seem in the making." (177)

After the stock market crash, the Federal Reserve System was evaluated respecting its share of blame in the catastrophe. In "What the Wall Street Crash Means", gold inflows from debtor nations and the increase in credit from the Federal Reserve allowed credit to expand faster than business. (178) The sterilization of gold imports had not occurred until vast quantities of gold had entered the country and had expanded credit. Security prices were consequently inflated, and:

"Business concerns as well as banks fed this inflation. Surplus business earnings were feed into the call market instead of being used for business expansion. Not only were current business needs financed by new security issues bought on bank credit, but the proceeds of such issues often went into further security loans. Corporations were thus engaged in a large scale in financing each others security issues." (179)

The Federal Reserve was unable to control the inflation because of the supply of foreign and domestic funds. *A fundamental cause of the crash, however, was that stock prices over anticipated the growth of American business.* The authors feared that once easy money came in again, speculative drives would be revitalized. Even the authors felt that the Federal Reserve had taken part in increasing credit. They also felt that foreign and corporation provided funds left the Board powerless to correct the situation.

Overall, bankers recommended that the discount rate be raised prior to the stock market crash, but they did not support the unfamiliar tax increase or security sales tools. Some businessmen, such as automobile entrepreneur, W. C. Durant, told the Federal Reserve to further lower the discount rate. He requested that the Board stay out of the credit situation. (180) Much of the financial community feared that the direct pressure tactics which the Federal Reserve System chose to adopt, instead of a discount rate hike, would cause panic. (Actually, the direct pressure tactics were not strong enough.)

When Charles Mitchell of the New York Federal Reserve Bank opposed the Federal Reserve Board, his resignation was requested. Bankers in defense of Mitchell asked why, when speculation had already run rampant for over a year, the Board chose now to warn against it. As we have seen, professional opinion placed a qualified blame on the Board after the crash. They recognized that business would have to suffer in order to halt the advance in security prices. (181)

In a book published in 1930, Professor Reed, whom we already have discussed as being in favor of general credit constriction, retrospectively analyzed the 1928-1929 speculative frenzy. (182) Prolonged credit restraint was again posited as the main requirement for restoring economic health. Reed, originally contrary to the idea of specifically limiting banks on security loans, now suggested that the situation could have been brought under control if the Federal Reserve had had the power to impose hefty discount charges on those banks with security loans. He defended the use of Reserve credit policy tools as he recognized that had they earlier and more zealously been employed, things would have been better. Reed, like his contemporaries, felt that after the stock market crash, the most important consideration was the restoration of general confidence. Reed applauded the Reserve Banks, their post market crash actions of purchasing government securities (increasing them from $17 million to $158 million), and their lowering of the discount rate. Reed commented:

"As a system designed to mitigate the intensity of money panics, the Reserve Banks again proved their worth and gained considerable prestige." (183)

Furthermore, while pointing out that others felt that the discount had been lowered too quickly, encouraging a new speculative boom, Reed felt that the rate drop had not been quick enough. He stated, "Depressions are drawn out longer than they need be simply because of the time required to get economic forces properly adjusted." (184)

In 1930, a particularly specific and detailed account of the Federal Reserve's policy was given in "The Stock Exchange Crisis of 1929". (185) This work reviewed the record of the Federal Reserve from July, 1927, until November, 1929. It concluded that two factors were evident. According to its author, Paul M. Warburg, a former Member of the Federal Reserve Board:

"One, the impressive demonstration of the System's structural strength, and two, the inadequacy of its form of administration." (186)

Warburg applauded the Federal Reserve System from preventing bank credit from becoming unstable after the market crash. Yet Warburg asserts:

"Why was it necessary, the historian will ask, for our financial authorities to stand by so long while unheard of quantities of inflammable material were massed in an unsafe structure, and while cool observers had been warning the public of the threatening, indeed, inevitable catastrophe?" (187)

In evaluating how responsible the Federal Reserve System was for the trauma at hand, Warburg first applauded the easing of the money supply in 1927 as a necessary measure to aid Europe, particularly Britain, in re-establishing the gold standard. As long as the Federal Reserve was prepared to reverse the policy once signs of over speculation or inflation appeared, Warburg felt this move to have been meritorious. While the System did at first take this appropriate corrective action in 1928, reversing this policy, in his opinion, was not done with "sufficient vigor and persistency" (188) because of the fear of harming business. Direct pressure tactics and even discount rate hikes proved insufficient as the Federal Reserve grappled ineffectively with competing desires of helping business and of restraining speculation. The Board's action in raising the discount rate at the New York bank to 6% on August 9, 1929, was at least one year too late, and Warburg pointed to a Board which sat immobile during the earlier, more critical months of 1929.

Businessmen, bankers, and government officials called for a halt in speculative activity, while politicians, economists, and financial leaders supported it as the new era. Direct pressure tactics were largely ineffectual as the bulk of the loans were from out of town banks, corporations, and foreign lenders. The Board should not have asked for lender cooperation, but borrower cooperation through stock exchange firms.

According to Warburg:

"If the Federal Reserve System and the clearing house banks had definitely agreed on the adoption of such a plan, the stock exchanges would have been forced to fall into line; for no matter how large a volume of funds stock exchange firms are receiving from "others", they would have realized that, in the final analysis, they were depending upon the strength and good will of New York banks... A procedure along these lines was definitely urged in the first days of April, 1929... The Reserve System feared to expose itself to the charge of having gone beyond its lawful field of activity by dealing even indirectly with the stock exchanges..." (189)

Warburg placed the blame for the lack of action on fact that the members of the Board itself were widely divided in opinion and rarely could agree on anything among themselves. Warburg further stated:

"The writer is profoundly convinced that with a different constitution of the Board, the ominous stock exchange debauch would have been arrested long before it reached its colossal dimensions." (190)

Warburg also felt that the laissez-faire, easy profit attitude of the country prevented the Board from acting. Congress also threatened the Board with nasty legislation if it actively entered the arena. All of these pressures, according to Warburg, "militated against the Board's doing what it should have done, which was to operate with clear vision, cool heads and a courageous disregard for all personal and political considerations." (192)

Concluding, 1929 was marked by some skepticism and on overly positive attitude toward future economic health. While some blame was placed on the Board for not constraining credit early enough, other independent factors such as foreign and corporation provided funds were cited to excuse the Federal Reserve Board. After the crash, the Board was blamed almost immediately. Probably the most detailed account of what went wrong was given in 1930 by Paul M. Warburg. He cited the following factors as most critical in the Board's failure to control the situation: easy money policy continuing too late into 1927, insufficient credit constraint in 1928, insufficient direct pressure tactics, inaction in raising the discount rate earlier, failure to appeal to stock exchange firms for constraint, Board Member disputes, and the fear of retaliation.

Therefore, it did not take long after the crash for the actual errors of the Federal Reserve Board clearly to be enunciated. Furthermore, warnings prior to the Great Crash were evident.

13. GENERAL ECONOMIC CONDITIONS (1930)

There are probably few who lived during the period who could forget 1930. After the stock market crash in October, 1929, a depression of international scope began to envelop the world. By 1930, this depression was world wide. Conditions at home were deteriorating rapidly. The first bank panic occurred in November, 1930. By December, 1930, 352 banks had been liquidated. In an attempt to rectify the situation, the Federal Reserve reduced the discount rate and conducted some open market purchases. However, as the months ahead proved, these attempts would have little impact in effectuating a recovery.

On January 1, 1930, in "1930-A Good But Not Easy Year", the depression was still referred to as a recession. (193) The business efficiency of 1929 was considered to be below par, with too much speculation, artificial conditions, and mergers. Farming was not expected to improve. Most city workers had to consume all of their paychecks in 1929 and were rapidly heading towards dissavings. A plea for credit expansion was also made. The article predicted:

"1930 won't be as good as 1929. As bad as 1924. A year of very cheap money. A year of record foreign trade. A bull market year. An easy year." (194)

By January, the swift corrective actions taken by the banks were applauded. (195) While recognizing that it was the banks in the financial centers which had bought loans thereby bailing out many brokers, writers stressed that: "...there is no reason to fear that serious trouble will arise anywhere in the United States or that dramatic action will be necessary." (196)

During the spring of 1930, the now noticeable bank failures were felt to be a normal response to the $25.7 million which the banks had paid out in the stock market crash. (198) Unemployment, declining commodity prices, and the freezing of many loans aggravated the situation. Rural banks were hurt by the movement of funds from rural to urban areas. Loan demand declines due to the "recession" of 1929-1930 further complicated the problem. It was claimed that some of the failed banks were so small that they never should have received state charters. In support of this contention, it was pointed out that failed banks in the South and West had average liabilities of $415,000 as compared with $3,000,000 nationally. Consequently, they had no tolerance for depressed conditions.

By July, 1930, brokers' loans had fallen dramatically from $3.4 billion to $371 million, the largest decline since the stock market crash. (198) Federal Reserve credit declined by $440 million, government securities declined by $20 million, and acceptance holdings declined by $30 million. Rediscounting climbed by $25 million. The article stated:

"The *Business Week* senses better times ahead for business now. The pessimistic stock market may not sense them for some time, but probably won't... Strong buying of the kind that is for "keeps" is in the market... The groundwork for large fortunes of the future is being laid, as many shrewd, small investors take advantage of stock prices the prediction of which would have been scorned a year from now and two years from now. Good judgment and selection are necessary and are being used." (199)

Businessmen angrily accused the "extreme conservatism" of both the banks and the Federal Reserve System for delaying economic recovery when by August, 1930, things had not improved. (200) The great caution of banking in choosing only the soundest issues of the bond market, the most liquid type of short term secondary investments, and secured loans was frowned upon. Bond prices reflected this shift in investment strategies with rising prices and lower yields. (201)

By November, 1930, the effects of the depression became manifest in a noticeably reduced growth in savings. (202) In fact, savings growth had fallen behind what banks had paid in interest.

The bond situation had turned around. In December, 1930, bond yields had climbed while prices had fallen. (203) The reasons given were general pessimism and that the banks (especially in New York) were selling industrial bonds and buying government bonds in order to obtain liquidity necessary to meet the strain of savings withdrawals. This selling contributed both to the decline in bond prices and to the lack of demand for bonds by insurance and other companies, investors, and savings banks. Fear of foreign instability and low corporate earnings continued to compound the problem. It was predicted that the weak bond market would in and of itself begin to hurt business, as an important source of investment funds was stiffled.

In "Upturn in Business in 1931 May Be Slow but Seems Sure", printed in the December 31, 1930 issue of *Business Week*, the economic downturn was referred to as a depression where things were expected to improve. (204) The following reasons were stated:

(1)   Business interruptions had never been long or severe in the past;

(2)   The depression was a cycle like other cycles and it should dissipate after approximately three months;

(3)   The positive attitude of businessmen was expected to improve the situation;

(4)   A surplus of investment funds would become available due to gold imports, return of currency from circulation, stock loan liquidation, the unusual liquidity of the banks, and the larger security holdings of the Federal Reserve Banks;

(5)   Replacement demand for obsolete or depleted items;

(6)   Increased consumer purchasing power arising from real income gains (the result of stable prices), social relief funds, public expenditures, debt liquidation, employment gains, and the payoff of installment loans. Borrowing from classic economic theories, it was believed that lower wages would lead to a greater level of employment.

In early 1931, Carl Snyder of the Federal Reserve Bank of New York stated that statistical measures indicated that the 1930 depression matched that of earlier periods of crisis such as 1877, 1893, 1907, and 1921. (205) Snyder felt this depression to be a business cycle for the United States and a severe calamity for the rest of the world. The overexpansion in the United States, once destroyed by the speculative mania, deeply hurt the rest of the world which was overly dependent on this country. Foreign countries were overdependent because the United States traditionally had imported large quantities of coffee, tea, sugar, cocoa, and industrial raw materials including rubber, and she had provided loans to them. Business writers maintained a very optimistic attitude in 1930 saying that while the economy was in an ill state of health, things were going to improve. Businessmen chided the Federal Reserve and banks in general for not bringing an immediate end to the situation. Classical theories of what was needed for recovery abounded.

14. FEDERAL RESERVE POLICY (1930)

According to the "Annual Report" of 1930, a policy of monetary ease was adopted in order to stimulate the slack activity in business. (206) In some cases, the Federal Reserve Banks reduced the discount rate to 2%. They also lowered the acceptance rate and purchased government securities. Gold imports from Latin America and the Orient also contributed to the easy money. The Federal Reserve noted the failure of many rural banks and a few city banks, and they attributed these failures to security and real estate operations. After the heavy, early gold exports to France and other countries, these countries returned to the gold standard and gold again flowed into the United States. In 1929, $228 million flowed in. In 1930, this trend continued for part of the year, and gold imports amounted to $345 million. During the course of 1930, loans and investments for trade and industry declined, but street loans actually increased as banks took them over after the market crash. The net result was a decrease of $1.05 billion in total loans and investments. The largest decreases were in rural banks. New York City loans and investments actually increased by $432 million. The Reserve stated that it would not comment on these problems as this was the task of various Congressional Committees established to review the situation.

In evaluating strategies available to the Federal Reserve System, three courses of action were given as possible. (207) First, open market operations could be used to ease money rates. Second, bills and securities could be sold to tighten credit and sterilize gold imports. Third, the Federal Reserve could permit gold imports to exert their natural easing influence. The article predicted that through open market operation and some manipulation of the discount rates, overall rates could be eased.

Economist A. C. Whitaker of Stanford University took the opportunity in the March, 1930, supplement of the *American Economic Review*, to commend the Federal Reserve for their performance to date:

"Despite the two great panic booms and collapses we have experienced since its foundation, one in the commodities and one in stocks, the Federal Reserve System is one of the most brilliant successes among our political and economic institutions... One of its chief difficulties is lack of control of what has been called the composition of the credit it extends. The Reserve banks may make their advances in strict accordance with law upon eligible commercial and government paper only, and yet the funds created may slip into the stock market. Another type of difficulty is conflict in the conditions to which the credit policy is to be adopted. Often one element in the state of affairs suggests strongly the policy of tightening money while another contemporaneously suggests the opposite." (208)

Whitaker also noted a very real problem facing the Federal Reserve. It did not have adequate securities available to make the potentially most powerful tool, open market operations, work. This was noted earlier in the paper, and it was a very significant problem. The conservative Federal Reserve did not even use all of the limited securities available. This point was stressed by *Business Week* in March. It was pointed out that Secretary Mellon was reducing the public debt so rapidly ($9 billion in 9 years) that not enough government securities were left. (209)

The use of open market operations was pleaded for by *Business Week*:

> "The system may resort to open market operations instead of changing the discount rate. These would be more effective and helpful to business in general than the rediscount rate change. Both actions are needed... The low level of business activity, calling for Federal Reserve help, is attested to in a number of ways." (210)

These "ways" included the decrease in member bank loans, the use of surplus finds to pay off Federal Reserve indebtedness, and a decrease in reserve credit outstanding to $1.08 billion.

Without placing judgment, *Business Week* also accounted for the recent problems facing the Federal Reserve. (211) *Business Week* reported that, according to the Federal Reserve, their greatest problem in 1929 was deterring the growth of security loans without hurting business. They did not want to raise the discount rate as they thought that to be too harsh a measure. So they asked for direct pressure on member banks. The Federal Reserve thought that that had outstanding results. While others thought that their delays, quibbling, and lack of decisiveness, as well as lack of forcefulness, in moving into individual banks had created the stock market crash. In defending themselves, the Federal Reserve added the use of direct pressure to their list of control measures for credit.

In June, 1930, Reynold Noyes criticized the Federal Reserve's handling of the gold inflows of 1922-1929. (212) These inflows produced a gigantic increase in bank credit which promptly entered the security markets, causing an inflation in the price of securities. Attempts to neutralize gold flows by substituting gold certificates (which did not count as reserves for Federal Reserve notes) in order to prevent bank credit expansion did not work. By enforcing credit expansion when it was needed, by paying undue attention to commodities and reviving business, instead of speculation, the Federal Reserve did more harm than good. New monetary policy, Noyes concluded, was required.

Finally, in the second half of 1930, commercial banks accused the Federal Reserve of delaying business recovery by doing "nothing". (213) In an effort to promote economic recovery, banks bought $350 in bonds over a period of several weeks. Meanwhile, commercial loans had plunged $100 million on one month. Borrowing on securities was shifting from brokers to banks, but banks thought that they were overall much too high. Approximately $50 million in gold was exported to Canada and France, and Federal Reserve credit dropped to $100 million, both factors making for tighter credit. According to *Business Week*:

"It is in purchases of government securities that the system has its only avenue to provide aid, since other channels are currently closed. Discount rates have been reduced adequately. This very action shows a halting idea by he system that something should be done. But discount rates are ineffective due to the extremely low level of borrowing." (214)

Therefore, while optimism for the future was retained throughout 1930 by businessmen, bankers, economists, and business writers, they generally agreed that open market operations needed to be conducted in order to restore stability. As was pointed out earlier, the Federal Reserve resisted offsetting gold exports with open market operations through most of 1932. When open market purchases were finally made in 1933, they were stopped short at a level below that which would effectuate needed help. The clear pleas of 1930 fell on deaf ears. Many banks would later pay for this with foreclosure. Federal Reserve inaction was the order of the day. *The Great Depression deepened.*

CHAPTER III

Conclusion
Policy Evaluation 1924-1930

The recession of 1924 was viewed by business writers that year as nearing its end. Business conditions did improve by the end of 1924. Meanwhile, the Federal Reserve was sterilizing gold inflows until they slowed in July, 1924. Policy was then reversed, open market purchases were made, and the discount rate was lowered. In easing money rates, the Federal Reserve stated that there was no evidence of a harmful growth in speculative activities. While bankers feared that inflation would be the result of easing measures, businessmen applauded them. At the same time other concerns were brought to the public's attention. Paul Warburg, a former member of the Federal Reserve Board, pointed to the dangers inherent in a Board comprised of laymen in the banking field who were also politically motivated. After the "Annual Report" of 1923, knowledgeable critics were aware of internal problems which would lead to debilitating problems later. The Federal Reserve ended its first year of real credit policy.

Prosperity was in full swing in 1925. Business writers were generally optimistic. Recognition of the dangers inherent in over speculation was evident. Foreboding words regarding the possible consequences of a boom were written. The Federal Reserve followed a policy of easy money, applauding the assistance that the United States was giving to the Europeans. In defending their policy of easy money, they explicitly stated that there was no dangerous speculative attitude. As usual, businessmen supported easy money and bankers feared inflationary consequences. Andrew Mellon, Secretary of the

Treasury, commended the Federal Reserve for their inestimable contributions to economic prosperity. Economists were not so clearly supportive. John R. Commons supported the sterilization policy. Economists Reed, Weyforth, and Beckhardt criticized the Reserve for fueling speculation and for their political motivations. The favoring of European interests above American interests was a matter of grave concern the these men. Weyforth warned that a severe depression was in store for the United States if the Federal Reserve did not begin to make moves toward restraining credit.

Speculation had overheated by 1926. The construction industry had saturated the post World War I market with homes and it had begun its decline. The attitude of business writers about the business expansion, the stock market, and speculation was optimistic until the latter half of 1926. Business writers warned against participation in stock market pools. By the end of the year, the slackening economy was described. A feeling that a minor market crash would rectify the situation in the near future was prevalent. In 1927, writing about 1926, the Federal Reserve viewed 1926 as a very healthy year meriting easy money. The predominantly rural, nonmember bank failures were blamed for poor internal management and insufficient capital, and were dismissed. The Federal Reserve noted the danger that rural bank runs had demonstrated. Apparently, however, they did not fear that these rural traumas could affect urban areas in any way. Bankers continued to criticize easy money policies, blaming the Federal Reserve for over speculation, and businessmen continued to applaud easy money. Governor Strong of the Federal Reserve Bank of New York noted the appropriateness of open market operations in affecting credit policy. He was supportive of the System. Some economists remained largely critical. Henry Chandler discussed the difficult issue facing the Reserve System in addressing both American and European needs without harming the credit structure. Henry Reed of Cornell University questioned sterilization of gold flow policies, easy money, and the use of securities markets to absorb the excesses. He angrily called for persistent reviews of the actions of what he considered to be an unqualified Board.

Another recession was evident by 1927. Business writers such as B. C. Forbes not only feared the stock market, but were aware that with the current recession it was unlikely that business would prosper sufficiently to catch up with (and warrant) the accelerated stock prices. Writers were also aware that certain abnormal factors such as the great post war construction activity would decline. The Federal Reserve reacted to the 1927 recession and the need by Europe for funds by conducting some open market purchases and by permitting the discount rate to slip by 1/2%. At the end of 1927, the Federal Reserve allowed gold exports to exert their contractionary influence on credit. The Federal Reserve found support by economists and business writers for these actions. Governor Benjamin strong was cited by everyone as the chief architect for Federal Reserve policy. However, Paul Warburg pointed to the need for the gradual removal of funds from the stock market, referring to the market as a "colossus" capable of causing a disaster. In 1929, Reed retrospectively analyzed 1927 stating that the catering to European interests was understandable in 1927. However, by August, 1927, he asserted that the Federal Reserve should have been able to see that conditions at home necessitated striking the balance in favor of the American economy through constraining credit. A month to month review of the situation at home might have led the Federal Reserve to this same conclusion.

In 1928, the Federal Reserve put the brakes on the booming market. *They did too little and they were too late.* Business writers rallied to support the prudent change in Federal Reserve policy, but they underestimated the gravity of the situation. They predicted a crash of high priced stocks and a return to a more rational market. The Federal Reserve defended its actions by saying that the change in credit policy, which they did not really effect until August, 1928, was initiated to curb credit expansion. Alluding to the conflicting domestic and foreign needs, the Federal Reserve stated that careful analysis of the advantages and disadvantages of their alternatives had to be weighed carefully. Support for the System was again divided, and O. M. Sprague of the Harvard Business School was aware that earlier restraining measures could have broken the bull market. He recommended that if a spectacular collapse of the securities market was in the offing, it would be better to withstand it sooner rather than to put it off until later.

The Great Crash of 1929 was built up to with some restraint of credit by the Federal Reserve, but with a relentless skyrocketing of all classes of security loans. After the crash, business writers were overly optimistic, calling the depression a case of dislocated seasonality. *Even though the Federal Reserve constrained credit still further, it was too little and too late. Their use of direct pressure tactics*

in asking member banks not to finance speculation would be ill-fated.
Economist Reed evaluated this as an error, as he felt that direct,
overall credit constraint was what was required. There was also an
awareness of the damaging role that the injection of surplus corporate
funds into the stock market had caused. Bickering with the New York
Federal Reserve Bank had also contributed to the stubborn refusal of
the Board in facilitating an increase in the discount rate. Reviewing
the 1929 situation in 1930, Paul Warburg placed initial blame on the
Federal Reserve Board for their lack of action in 1928. He felt that
the easy money policies of 1927 may have worked to the benefit of
Europe without hurting domestic interests had this policy been
reversed immediately and decisively in 1928, once excess speculation
was ready to cause a collapse. He continued his criticism of the
Board's bickering, political motivations, and lack of mobilization at the
appropriate time.

Business writers of 1930 still viewed the depression as a
recession, but toward the end of 1930 opinions became gloomier. The
Federal Reserve initially reacted to the situation by by easing credit
and they refused comment on the 1930 bank failures other than stating
that they were not the Board's responsibility. The fact that the Federal
Reserve was not making fuller use of government securities in the
form of open market purchases was criticized by business writers,
bankers, and economists. Their pleas for open market operations fell
on deaf ears at the Board, and even when in 1932 open market
operations were conducted, they were too brief and too small to help
significantly.

Concluding, then, the first ten years of Federal Reserve credit
policy led to drastic and damaging results. Led by a man who
presumably understood the appropriate use of credit policy, Benjamin
Strong promoted easy money conditions in an effort to help Europe.
Whether he would have insisted on a forceful reversal of expansion
policy, given both his desire to promote worldwide stability and his
understanding of credit policy tools, is unknown because of his death
in 1928. Economists of that era seemed to feel that had action been
taken to restrain credit expansion from mid 1927 through early 1928 in
a sufficiently forceful manner, the inevitable boom-to-bust might have
been less dramatic. It is the opinion of this writer that the actions of
the Federal Reserve Board were understandable until August, 1927,
given conflicting domestic and foreign interests and political pressures
rendering the Board amenable to everything to promote business.

However, beyond that point, their bickering and indecisiveness led the Board to an inexcusable continuance of easy money. After the crash of the stock market, it was apparent that an easing of credit was needed. Then, the Federal Reserve showed very poor judgment in refusing to use open market operations, the most effective credit policy tool. When eased credit was needed after the crash, a refusal to use this most effective of their credit policy tools, open market operations, showed very poor judgment. How the Board could refuse to steer a clear course from mid 1927, when the objective opinions of bankers, business writers, and economists were clear and convincing, is difficult to grasp. The pleading voices of leaders of industry and Europeans for continued easy money must have been heeded in the first instance. Then a gun shy attitude towards easing credit must have guided the Board after the Great Crash.

It is true that neither the strict Keynesian nor the the Monetarist views of the causes of the Great Depression has been accepted uniformly. The truth probably lies somewhere in between. The role that the Federal Reserve System played during the onset of the depression, and the maintenance of the tragedy, posits a lesson for history regarding the dangers of powerful, less than competent, politically motivated, and divided Systems.

BIBLIOGRAPHY

Books

Chandler, Lester V., *America's Greatest Depression 1929-1941,* (New York: Harper-Row Publishing, 1970).

Fite, Gilbert C., and Reese, Jim E., *An Economic History of the United States,* (Boston: Houghton Mifflin Co., 1965).

Friedman, Milton K., and Schwartz, Anna Jacobsen, *A Monetary History of the United States 1867-1960,* (Princeton: Princeton University Press, 1963).

Galbraith, John, *The Great Crash of 1929,* (New York: Time Inc., 1954).

Hacker, Louis M., *The Course of American Growth and Economic Development,* (New York: John Wiley Sons, Inc., 1970).

Kroose, Herman E., *Executive Opinion What Business Leaders Said and Thought on Economic Issues 1920's-1960's,* (New York: Doubleday and Co., Inc., 1970). .

Lee, Susan Previant and Passell, Peter, *A New Economic View of American History,* (New York: W.W. Norton Co., 1979).

Niemi, Albert W. Jr., *U.S. Economic History,* (Chicago: Rand McNally Publishing Co., 1981).

O'Sullivan, John, and Keuchel, Edward F., *American   Economic History From Abundance to Constraint,* (New York: Franklin Watts Publishing, 1981).

Reed, Harold L., *Federal Reserve Policy 1921-1930,* (New York: McGraw-Book Co., Inc., 1930).

Temin, Peter, *Did Monetary Forces Cause the Great Depression,* (New York: W.W. Norton Inc., 1976).

Warburg, Paul M., *The Federal Reserve System Its Origin and Growth-Reflections and Recollections, Volumes One and Two,* (New York: Address and Essays, 1930).

Periodicals

Burgess, W. Randolph, "The Reserve Banks and the New York Money Market", *American Bankers Association Journal,* (April 1926), 669-672.

Burgess, W. Randolph, "What the Federal Reserve System is Doing to Promote Business Stability", *Proceeding of the Academy of Political Science,* (July 1927), 139-148.

Business Week, "1930-A Good but not Easy Year", (January 1, 1930), 20.

Business Week, "Banking in 1930", (January 1, 1930), 25.

Business Week, "Bankers Demand Loan Investigation", (October 5, 1929), 17.

Business Week, "Bankers are Puzzled by Problem of Investing New Savings", (October 15, 1930), 16.

Business Week, "Bonds Drop to New Low Levels Defying Every Market Precedent", (December 24, 1930), 5.

Business Week, "Business Outlook-Clearing, Continued Cool", (November 2, 1929), 3.

Business Week, "Business Outlook Fair but Cooler", (September 7, 1929), 3.

Business Week, "Business Outlook-Unsettled Slightly Warmer", (October 5, 1929), 9.

Business Week, "Business Sees Recovery Braked by Overcautious Bankers", (August 20, 1930), 17.

Business Week, "Current Bank Failures Include Many Postpones Last Year", (April 23, 1930), 12.

Business Week, "Federal Reserve Board Makes Direct Pressure Fixed Policy", (May 7, 1930), 11.

Business Week, "Federal Reserve Inactivity Helps Delay Business Upturn", (August 6, 1930), 10.

Business Week, "In the Opinion of 5600 Businessmen", (October 5, 1929), 27.

Business Week, "Money and Market", (September 14, 1929): 22.

Business Week, "Money and Market", (October 5, 1929), 20.

Business Week, "Money and the Market", (October 19, 1929): 20.

Business Week, "Money and the Market", (July 2, 1930), 36.

Business Week, "Money and the Market", (February 26, 1930), 20.

Business Week, "Money and the Market", (March 12, 1930), 19.

Business Week, "Savings Growth Falls Short of Sum Banks Paid in Interest", (November 12, 1930), 7.

Business Week, "Should the Reserve Lower the Bars", (March 5, 1930), 35.

Business Week, "Upturn of Business in 1931 May Be Slow But Seems Sure", (December 31, 1930), 9.

Business Week, "What Kind of Business Recession", (December 11, 1929), 20.

Business Week, "What the Wall Street Crash Means", (November 2, 1929), 20.

Business Week, "World Credit Tangle No Nearer Solution", (October 12, 1929), 6.

Cargill Thomas F., "The Great Depression and the Monetarist Debate", University of Nevada at Reno, (1981).

Chandler, Henry A.E., "Power of the Reserve Banks to Control Credit", *Commerce Monthly*, (February 1926), 3-10.

Commons, John R., "Price Stabilization and the Federal Reserve", *The Annalist*, (April 1, 1927), 459-462.

Donley J.G., "Will Decline in Stocks be Reflected in Business", *Forbes Magazine*, (November 1, 1926), 7.

Forbes, B.C., "Are 2,000,000 Share Days and Business Expansion Justified", *Forbes Magazine*, (December 15, 1924), 331.

Forbes, B. C., "Are Stocks Dangerously High?", *Forbes Magazine*, (September 1, 1925), 725.

Forbes, B. C., "B. C. Forbes Analyzes Bull Market and Sounds Warning", *Forbes Magazine*, (May 1, 1928), 11.

Forbes, B. C., "B. C. Forbes Cites Favorable and Unfavorable Factors Deductions Drawn", *Forbes Magazine*, (September 1, 1928), 11.

Forbes, B. C., "B. C. Forbes Sees Betterment in Business", *Forbes Magazine*, (February 15, 1928), 7.

Forbes, B. C., "B. C. Forbes Thinks Money Will Force Stocks Down", *Forbes Magazine*, (June 15, 1928), 11.

Forbes B. C., "Business and Stock Market Very Happy-Will it Last", *Forbes Magazine*, (October 1, 1925), 869.

Forbes B. C., "Business and Stocks Move Very Unevenly", *Forbes Magazine*, (Novewmber 15, 1927), 7.

Forbes B. C., "Business Is Sounder than the Stock Market", *Forbes Magazine*, (December 1, 1925), 7.

Forbes B. C., "Business Outlook for Second Half of 1927", *Forbes Magazine*, (June 1, 1927), 7.

Forbes, B. C., "Collapse of Stock Pools Not Due to Business", *Forbes Magazine*, (March 15, 1926), 7.

Forbes B. C., "Decided Change in Business Looked for Shortly", *Forbes Magazine*, (February 2, 1924), 497.

Forbes B. C., "Has Stock Speculation Become Dangerous", *Forbes Magazine*, (August 15, 1926), 7.

Forbes, B. C., "Prices are Declining Wages are Rising Yet", *Forbes Magazine*, (November 1, 1926), 7.

Forbes, B C., "These 25 Developments Justify Confidence", *Forbes Magazine*, (March 1, 1926), 7.

Forbes, B. C., "Why Confidence is Returning", *Forbes Magazine*, (May 15, 1926), 7.

Forbes, B. C., "Will We Handle the Elements of Prosperity Prudently", *Forbes Magazine*, (January 15, 1925), 445.

Forbes Magazine, "Fact and Comment: Unhealthy Speculation in the Stock Market", (August 15, 1926), 7.

Forbes Magazine, "Forbes Time Saving News Service", (December 1, 1926), 53.

Gordon, Robert J., and Wilcox, James A., "Monetarist Interpretation of the Great Depression: An Evaluation and Critique", *Center for Research in Government Policy and Business*, (1978).

Jaeger, E. V., "When Will Stocks Reach Peak", *Forbes Magazine*, (February 1, 1926), 63.

Lewis, Reuben A., "The Open Market Operations of the Federal Reserve System", *American Bankers Association Journal*, (May 1926), 742-744.

McNeel, R. W., "Permanent Prosperity is it a Sure Thing?", *Forbes Magazine*, (August 1, 1928), 15.

Mellon, Andrew W., "What Future for the Federal Reserve", *Nation's Business*, (May 1925).

Moody, John, "Modern Investor Has the Nation-the-World at His Feet", *Forbes Magazine*, (October 15, 1924), 79.

Noyes, Reinnold C., "Gold Inflation in U. S. 1921-1929", *The American Economic Review*, (June, 1930), 181-198.

Oakwood, John, "Are the Days of High Money Rates Gone Forever", *Forbes Magazine*, (November 1, 1925), 78.

Oakwood, John, "Truth About Bank Failures in the Northwest", *Forbes Magazine*, (March 1, 1924), 629.

Reed, H. L., "The Recent Work of the Federal Reserve Administration", *The American Economic Review*, (March, 1926), 303-314.

Rukeyser, Merryl Stanly, "America Faces Gold Outflow to Europe", *Forbes Magazine*, (January 15, 1926), 14.

Schabacker, R. W., "Firmer Credit a Bugaboo Only to Speculation", *Forbes Magazine*, (March 1, 1928), 7.

Sprague, O. M. W., "Broker's Loans Dangerous-Reserve Banks Largely Responsible for Inflation", *The Annalist*, (April 20, 1928), 687.

Weyforth, W. O., "The Retirement of National Bank Notes", *The Journal of Political Economy*, (October 25), 545.

Whitaker, A. C., "Federal Reserve Position and Policies", *The American Economic Review*, (March Supplement 1930), 97.

Young, Allyn A., "The Control of the Federal Reserve System", *The Annalist*, (May 6, 1927), 643-645.

Young, Honorable Roy A., "Federal Reserve Policies and the Present Credit Situation", *Trust and Estates*, (September 1928), 280-282.

Government Publications

"Eleventh Annual Report of The Federal Reserve Board Covering Operations for the Year 1924", (Washington: Government Printing Office, 1925), 10-12.

"Twelfth Annual Report of the Federal Reserve Board Covering Operations for the Year 1925", (Washington: Government Printing Office, 1926), 1-7.

"Thirteenth Annual Report of the Federal Reserve Board Covering Operations for the Year 1926", (Washington: Government Printing Office, 1927), 13.

"Fourteenth Annual Report of the Federal Reserve Board Covering Operations for the Year 1927", (Washington: Government Printing Office, 1928), 1-20.

"Fifteenth Annual Report of the Federal Reserve Board Covering Operations for the Year 1928", (Washington: Government Printing Office, 1929), 1-19.

"Sixteenth Annual Report of the Federal Reserve Board Covering Operations for the Year 1929", (Washington: Government Printing Office, 1930), 2.

"Seventeenth Annual Report of the Federal Reserve Board Covering Operations for the Year 1930", (Washington: Government Printing Office, 1931), 1-12.

"Federal Reserve Bulletin 1924", Volume X, (New York: Kraus Reprint Corporation, 1965), 243-251.

"Federal Reserve Bulletin 1925", (Washington: Government Printing Office, 1925), 7.

NOTES

1.   Fite, Gilbert C. and Reese, Jim E., *An Economic History of the United States,* (Boston: Houghton Mifflin Company, 1965), 529.

2.   Fite, 538.

3.   Fite, 537-538.

4.,   Fite, 542.

5.   Fite, 542.

6.   Fite, 544.

7.   Fite, 542.

8.   Fite, 531.

9.   Niemi, Albert W. , Jr., *U.S. Economic History,* (Chicago: Rand McNally Publishing Co., 1981), 384.

10.   Hacker, Louis M., *The Course of American Growth and Development,* (New York: John Wiley and Sons, Inc., 1970), 286.

11.   Friedman, Milton K., and Schwartz, Anna Jacobsen, *A Monetary History of the United States,* (Princeton: Princeton University Press, 1963), 240-241.

12.   Friedman, 298.

13.   Niemi, 383.

14.   Hacker, 274-299.

15.   Fite, 528-590.

16.   Galbraith, John, *The Great Cash 1929,* (New York: Times, Inc., 1954).

17.   Lee, Susan Previant and Passell, Peter, *A New Economic View of American History,* (New York: W.W. Norton and Co., 1979), 362-392.

18.   Hacker, 288.

19.   Fite, 557.

20.   Fite, 557.

21.   Hacker, 275-320.

22.   Lee, 339.

23.   Fite, 506.

24.   O'Sullivan, John and Keuchel, Edward F., *American Economic History From Abundance to Constraint,* (New York: Franklin Watts Publishing 1981), 166.

25.   Fite, 506.

26.   O'Sullivan, 165.

27.   O'Sullivan, 165.

28.   Hacker, 293.

29.   Chandler, Lester V., *American Economic Growth and Development,* (New York: Harper and Row Publishers 1970), 18.

30.   Hacker, 292.

31.   Hacker, 292.

32.   Friedman, 244.

33.   Friedman, 245.

34.   Friedman, 249.

35.   Friedman, 249.

36.   Friedman, 249.

37.   Friedman, 50-52.

38.   Friedman, 283.

39.   Friedman, 283.

40.   Friedman, 284.

41.   Friedman, 288.

42.   Friedman, 288.

43.   Friedman, 297.

44.   Galbraith, 32.

45.   Friedman, 260.

46.   Galbraith, 32-55.

47.   Friedman, 299.

48.   Chandler, 6.

49.   Chandler, 6.

50.   Chandler, 2.

51.   Friedman, 301-305.

52.   Chandler, 20-22.

53.   Fite, 583.

54.   Chandler, 20-22.

55.   Friedman, 305.

56.   Friedman, 335.

57.   Friedman, 339-340.

58.   Friedman, 308.

59.   Friedman, 308-313.

60.   Friedman, 313.

61.   Friedman, 315.

62.   Friedman, 346.

63.   Friedman, 349.

64.   Chandler, 260.

65.   Friedman, 351.

66.   Friedman, 358.

67.   Temin, Peter, *Did Monetary Forces Cause the Great Depression,* (New York: W.W. Norton Inc., 1976), 82.

68.   Temin, 82.

69.   Gordon, Robert J., and Wilcox, James A., *Montarist Interpretation of the Great Depression,* (Center for Research in Government Policy and Business, 1978).

70.   Cargill, Thomas F., *The Great Depression and the Montarist Debate,* (University of Nevada at Reno, 1981).

71.   Fite, 538-539.

72.   Forbes, B.C., "Decided Change in Business", *Forbes Magazine,* (February 2, 1924), 497.

73.   Forbes, B.C., 497.

74.   Forbes, B.C., "Are 2,000,000-Share Days and Business Expansion Justified", *Forbes Magazine,* (December 15, 1924), 331.

75.   Forbes, B.C., 331.

76.   Moody, John, "Modern Investor Has the Nation-the-World at His Feet", *Forbes Magazine,* (October 15, 1924), 79.

77.   Oakwood, John, "Truth About Bank Failures in the Northwest", *Forbes Magazine,* (March 1, 1924), 629.

78.   Oakwood, John, 629.

79.   Oakwood, John, 629.

80.   "Federal Reserve Bulletin 1924, Volume X", (New York: Kraus Reprint Corportation (1965), 243-251.

81.   "Federal Reserve Bulletin 1924", 685.

82.   "Annual Report of the Federal Reserve Board Covering Operations for the Year 1924", (Washington: Government Printing Office 1925), 10-12.

83.   "Annual Report of the Federal Reserve Board Covering Operations for the Year 1924", (Washington: Government Printing Office 1925), 10-12.

84.   "Federal Reserve Bulletin 1924", 685.

85.   Krooss, Herman E., *Executive Opinion What Bussiness Leaders Said and Thought on Economic Issues 1920's-1960's,* (New York: Doubleday and Co., Inc., 1970), 84-87.

86.   Warburg, Paul M., *The Federal Reserve System It's Origin and Groth,* (New York: The Macmillan Co., 1930), 843-854.

87.   Fite, 538-539.

88.   Forbes, B.C., "Will We Handle the Elements of Prosperity Prudently?", *Forbes Magazine*, (January 15, 1925), 445.

89.   Forbes B.C., "Are Stocks Dangerly High?", *Forbes Magazine*, (October 1, 1925), 927.

90.   Forbes B.C.,"Business and Stock Market Very Happy Will it Last?", *Forbes Magazine*, (September 1, 1925), 725.

91.   Forbes B.C., 725.

92.   Oakwood, John, "Are the Days of High Money Rates Gone Forever?", *Forbes Magazine*, (November 1, 1925), 34.

93.   Oakwood, John. 34.

94.   Forbes B.C., "Business Is Sounder then Stock Market", *Forbes Magazine*, (December 1, 1925), 7.

95.   "Federal Reserve Bulletin 1925", (Washington: Government Printing Office,1925) 71-74.

96.   "Twelfth Annual Report of the Federal Reserve Board Covering Operations for the Year 1925", (Washington: Government Printing Office, 1926), 1-7.

97. "Twelfth Annual Report of the Federal Reserve Board Covering Operations for the Year 1925", 6.

98. Krooss, Herman E., "The Money Supply and Credit", *Executive Opinion What Business Leaders Said and Thought on Economic Issues 1920's-1960's,* (New York: Doubleday and Company, Inc. 1970), 78-80.

99. Mellon, Andrew W., "What Future for the Federal Reserve?", *Nation's Business*, (May 1925), 46.

100. Mellon, Andrew W., 46,

101. Commons, John R., "The Stablization of Prices and Business", *American Economic Review* (March 1925), 43-52.

102. Krooss, 78-80.

103. Weyforth, W.O., "The Retirement of the National Bank Notes"*The Journal of Political Economy*, (October, 1925), 545.

104. Fite, 538.

105. Fite, 539.

106. Jaeger, E.V., "When Will Stocks Reach Peak?", *Forbes Magazine*, (March 15, 1926), 7.

107. Forbes B.C., "These 25 Developments Justify Confidence", *Forbes Magazine*, (March 1, 1926), 7.

108. Forbes B.C., "Collapse of Stock Pools Not Due to Business", *Forbes Magazine*, (March 15, 1926), 7.

109. Forbes B.C., "Why Confidence Is Returning", *Forbes Magazine*, (May 15, 1926), 7.

110. Forbes B.C. ,"Has Stock Speculation Become Dangerous", *Forbes Magazine*, (August 15, 1926), 7.

111.   "Fact and Comment: Unhealthy Speculation in the Stock Market", *Forbes Magazine*, (September 15, 1926), 28.

112.   "Forbes Time Saving News Service", *Forbes Magazine*, (December 1, 1926), 53.

113.   "Thirteenth Annual Report of the Federal Reserve Board Covering Operations for the Year 1926", (Washington: U. S. Government Printing Office, 1927), 13.

114.   Krooss, 95-99.

115.   Chandler, 3-10.

116.   Reed, H.L., "The Recent Work of the Federal Reserve Administration", *The American Economic Review*, Volume 16, (March 1926), 303-315.

117.   Reed, 331.

118.   Burgess, W. Randolph, "The Reserve Banks and the New York Money Marker", *American Banker's Association Journal*, (May 1926), 742-744.

119.   Lewis, Reuben A., "The Open Market Operations of the Federal Reserve System", *American Banker's Association Journal*, (May 1926), 742-744.

120.   Donley, J.G., "Will Decline in Stocks be Reflected in Business?", *Forbes Magazine*, (November 1, 1926), 7.

121.   Fite, 538-539.

122.   Forbes B.C., "Prices are Declining Wages are Rising Yet", *Forbes Magazine*, (April 1, 1927), 7.

123.   Forbes B.C., "Business Outlook for Second Half of 1927", *Forbes Magazine*, (June 1, 1927), 7.

124. Forbes B.C., "Business and Stocks Move Very Unevenly", *Forbes Magazine*, (August 1, 1927), 15.

125. McNell, R.W., "Permant Prosperity is it a Sure Thing", *Forbes Magazine*, (August 1, 1927), 15.

126. "Fourteenth Annual Report of the Federal Reserve Board Covering Operations for the Year 1927", (Washington: U.S. Governement Printing Office, 1928),1-20.

127. "Fourteenth Annual Report of the Federal Reserve Board Covering Operations for the Year 1927", 6.

128. "Fourteenth Annual Report of the Federal Reserve Board Covering Operations for the Year 1927", 10.

129. "Fourteenth Annual Report of the Federal Reserve Board Covering Operations for the Year 1927", 12.

130. Young, Allyn A., "The Control of the Federal Reserve System", *The Annalist*, (May 6, 1927), 643-645.

131. Commons, John R., "Price Stabilization and the Federal Reserve System", *The Annalist*, (Aprill 1, 1927), 459-462.

132. Rukeyser, Merryle Stanley, "American Faces Fold Outflow to Europe", *Forbes Magazine*, (January 15, 1927), 14.

133. Burgess, W.R., "What the Federal Reserve System is Doing to Promote Business Stability", *Proceedings of the Academy of Political Science*, (July 1927), 139-148.

134. Burgess, 140.

135. Warburg, 458.

136. Reed, Harold L., *Federal Reserve Policy 1921-1930*, (New York: McGraw-Hill Book Co., Inc., 1930), 78-203.

137. Fite, 538-539.

138.   Forbes B.C., "Forbes Sees Betterment in Business", *Forbes Magazine*, (March 1, 1928), 7.

139.   Schabacker, R.W., "Firmer Credit a Bugaboo Only to Speculation", *Forbes Magazine*, (March 1, 1928), 7.

140.   Forbes B.C., "B.C. Forbes Analyze Bull Market and Sounds Warning", *Forbes Magazine*, (May 1, 1928), 11.

141.   Forbes B.C., 11.

142.   Forbes B.C., "B.C. Forbes Thinks Money Will Force Stocks Down", *Forbes Magazine*, (June 15, 1928), 11.

143.   Forbes B.C., "B.C. Forbes Cites Favorable and Unfavorable Factors Deductions Drawn", *Forbes Magazine*, (September 1, 1928), 11.

144.   "Fifteenth Annual Report of the Federal Reserve Board Covering Operations for the Year 1928", (Washington: U.S. Government Printing Office, 1929), 1-19.

145.   "Fifteenth Annual Report of the Federal Reserve Board Covering Operations for the Year 1928", 8.

146.   "Fifteenth Annual Report of the Federal Reserve Board Covering Operations for the Year 1928", 9.

147.   Krooss, 101-106.

148.   Young, Honorable Roy A., "Federal Reserve Policies and the Present Credit Situation", *Trusts and Estates*, (September 1928), 280-282.

149.   Sprague, O.M.W., "Broker's Loans Dangerous--Reserve Banks Largely Responsible for Inflation", *The Annalist*, (April 20, 1928), 687.

150.   Warburg, 869-871.

151. Fite, 538-539.

152. Fite, 542.

153. Fite, 557.

154. O'Sullivan, 166.

155. Hacker, 293.

156. Hacker, 292.

157. Friedman, 284.

158. Friedman, 284..

159. Friedman, 305.

160. "Business Outlook-Fair but Cooler", *Business Week*, (September 7, 1929), 3.

161. "Money and Market", *Business Week*, (September 14, 1929), 22.

162. "Business Outlook, Unsettled Slightly Warmer", *Business Week*, (October 5, 1929), 3.

163. "Bankers Demand Loan Investigation", *Business Week*, (October 5, 1929), 17.

164. "Money and the Market", *Business Week*, (October 5, 1929), 20.

165. "In the Opinion of 5600 Businessmen", *Business Week*, (October 5, 1929), 27.

166. "In the Opinion of 5600 Businessmen", 27.

167. "Money and the Market", 20.

168.   "Business Outlook-Clearing, Continued Cool", *Business Week*, (November 2, 1929), 3.

169.   "What the Wall Street Crash Means", *Business Week*, (November 2, 1929), 20.

170.   "What Kind of Business Recession", *Business Week*, (December 11, 1929), 20.

171.   "Sixteenth Annual Report of the Federal Reserve Board Covering Operations for the Year 1929", (Washington: U.S. Government Printing Office, 1930), 2.

172.   "Sixteenth Annual Report of the Federal Reserve Board Covering Operations for the Year 1929", 2.

173.   "Sixteenth Annual Report of the Federal Reserve Board Covering Operations for the Year 1929", 4.

174.   "Sixteenth Annual Report of the Federal Reserve Board Covering Operations for the Year 1929", 4.

175.   Reed, 78-90.

176.   "World Credit Triangle No Nearer Solution", *Business Week*, (October 12, 1929), 6.

177.   "World Credit Triangle No Nearer Solution", 6.

178.   "What the Wall Street Crash Means", 20.

179.   "What the Wall Street Crash Means", 22.

180.   Krooss, 107.

181.   Krooss, 103.

182.   Reed, 154-192.

183.   Reed, 187.

184. Reed, 191.

185. Warburg, 501-517.

186. Warburg, 501.

187. Warburg, 502.

188. Warburg, 504.

189. Warburg, 511.

190. Warburg, 514.

191. Warburg, 514.

192. Friedman, 308.

193. "1930-a Good but not Easy Year", *Business Week*, (January 1, 1930), 20.

194. "1930-a Good but not Easy Year", 20.

195. "Banking in 1930", *Business Week*, (January 1, 1930), 25.

196. "Banking In 1930", 25.

197. "Current Bank Failures Include Many Postponed Last Year", *Business Week*, (April 23, 1930), 12.

198. "Money and the Market", *Business Week*, (July 2, 1930), 36.

199. "Money and the Market", 36.

200. "Business Sees Recovery Braked by Overcautions Bankers", *Business Week*, (April 23, 1930), 17.

201. "Banks are Puzzled by Problem of Investing New Savings", *Business Week*, (October 15, 1930), 16.

202.   "Savings Growth Falls Short of Sum Banks Paid in Interest",
Business Week, (November 12, 1930), 7.

203.   "Bonds Drop to New Low Levels Defying Every Market
Precedent", *Business Week*, (December 24, 1930), 5.

204.   "Upturn of Business in 1931 May be Slow but Seams Sure",
Business Week, (December 31, 1930), 9.

205.   "Seventeenth Annual Report of the Federal Reserve Board
Covering Operations For the Year 1930", (Washington: U.S.
Government Printing Office, 1931), 1-12.

206.   "Seventeenth Annual Report of the Federal Reserve Board
Covering Operations For the Year 1930", 1-12.

207.   "Money and the Market", *Business Week*, (February 26, 1930),
20.

208.   Whitaker, A.C., "Federal Reserve Position and Policies", *The
American Economic Review*, Volume 20, No. 1 ,(1930), 97.

209.   "Should the Reserve Lower the Bars", *Business Week*, (March
5, 1930), 35.

210.   "Money and the Market", *Business Week*, (March 12, 1930),
19.

211.   "Federal Reserve Board Makes Direct Pressure Fixed Policy",
Business Week, (May 7, 1930), 11.

212.   Noyes, Reinold C., "Gold Inflation in U.S. 1921-1929", *The
American Economic Review*, (June, 1930), 181-198.

213.   "Federal Reserve's Inactivity Helps Delay Business Upturn",
Business Week, (August 6, 1930), 10.

214.   "Federal Reserve's Inactivity Helps Delay Business Upturn",
10.

For Product Safety Concerns and Information please contact our EU
representative GPSR@taylorandfrancis.com Taylor & Francis Verlag GmbH,
Kaufingerstraße 24, 80331 München, Germany

Printed and bound by CPI Group (UK) Ltd, Croydon, CR0 4YY
08/05/2025
01864439-0004